Margaret Withers took up her role as the Archbishop's Officer for Evangelism among Children in June 2001. Formerly Children's Work Adviser for the Diocese of Rochester, she taught in several Inner London schools and for the Open University before becoming a Diocesan Children's Adviser in 1989. During her years as a Diocesan Adviser, she became heavily involved in providing training and support for voluntary children's leaders in parishes. In 1996, while Children's Officer for the diocese of Chelmsford, she established children's work as an integral part of Reader training as well as providing a similar input to several theological courses. The increasing demand for simple basic training for inexperienced leaders led to her writing a four-evening course for a group of parishes in 1998. This formed the basis of her book Fired Up... Not Burnt Out, which was published under BRF's Barnabas imprint in 2001. She is also author of The Gifts of Baptism and Welcome to the Lord's Table, both also published under the Barnabas imprint.

Text copyright © Margaret Withers 2005
The author asserts the moral right
to be identified as the author of this work

Published by
The Bible Reading Fellowship
First Floor, Elsfield Hall
15–17 Elsfield Way, Oxford OX2 8FG

ISBN 1 84101 361 7
First published 2005
10 9 8 7 6 5 4 3 2 1 0

Acknowledgments
Unless otherwise stated, scripture quotations are taken from the
Contemporary English Version of the Bible published by HarperCollins
Publishers, copyright © 1991, 1992, 1995 American Bible Society.

A catalogue record for this book is available from the British Library

Printed and bound in Great Britain by
Bookmarque, Croydon

WHERE ARE THE CHILDREN?

Evangelism beyond Sunday morning

MARGARET WITHERS

ACKNOWLEDGMENTS

Thanks are due to:

The Revd Ian Gibson of Unlimited Potential for the use of his material on management of change in Chapter 7, 'Change and act'.

The Revd John Guest, Rector of St Margaret's, Stanford le Hope, for allowing me to reproduce his article 'Building Bridges' from my mailing, REACH (Resourcing Evangelism among Children).

The Revd Martin Leigh, vicar of St Edward's, Cheddleton, for introducing me to the KOS (Kids on Saturdays) club.

Judith Wigley, Youth and Children's Networker in Otley Deanery and former Adviser for under fives in the diocese of Wakefield, for her story 'The Confirmation' and her knowledge and enthusiasm for a ministry with very young children.

Colleagues in the dioceses of Chelmsford and Rochester for giving me inspiration, information, and examples of the way that they enable children to hear the gospel message.

Last, but not least, 'Joseph' who I met briefly in Deptford in 1994 and whose story has humbled and encouraged me ever since.

CONTENTS

FOREWORD

When Jesus welcomed children to listen to him and spend time with him, the Gospels don't suggest that he was either simply baby-sitting or keeping them amused on the off-chance that they might be useful members of the Church later on. On the contrary, he speaks of his 'little followers', 'little ones who believe in me'. And our engagement, as not-so-little followers, with children has to be equally serious, equally a matter of shared life, not patronizing control.

Margaret Withers gives us a superb overview of what is happening and what could be happening in our churches to take this forward. She reminds us that the Church's involvement with children is currently developing in really encouraging ways, and offers practical and imaginative proposals for a ministry that does indeed take children seriously. She lists various styles of work, and resources of all sorts that can be deployed to put them into effect. She warns against overestimating what can be done, but makes it very clear that clarity about the task can help you make astonishingly creative use of even the most apparently meagre resources. She even provides helpful (and necessary) advice on the sort of songs that work with children, and on the problems of dealing with mixed age groups.

This is in every way a heartening and invigorating book that will be a godsend for all kinds of churches. I hope that it will nourish still further the rapidly expanding scope of our sharing the gospel with children—and our hearing the gospel from them.

+ *Rowan Cantuar*

INTRODUCTION

Where are the Children? is designed to help you and your fellow Christians to explore ways of enabling children to hear the good news of God in Christ. During the last 20 years, most churches have focused their ministry with children on providing nurture during the Sunday morning service. Worshipping as the Lord's family on the Lord's Day is vital but, with a rapidly changing and mobile society, it is essential to reach out to children in other ways and within the local community. It is equally important to recognize and celebrate the worship that is going on at other times and in other places, in Church schools, at parent and toddler groups, in holiday clubs and some uniformed organizations. The list is endless but these other ways of being Church often remain unnoticed and unreported.

In 1991, the Church of England published a report, *All God's Children?* with the stark sub-title, 'Children's Evangelism in Crisis'.[1] It stated that only 15 per cent of children aged less than 13 years were involved in church-related activities. It questioned whether Sunday was the best day on which to reach unchurched children. It explored the relationship between a church and its local schools and the value of uniformed organizations. Since then, the child's world has changed radically, but the issues remain.

Since that report was published, thousands of youngsters have attended church-led holiday clubs, pre-schools and toddler groups. Children are more involved in Sunday worship, including the Eucharist. Some schools have started to form links with local churches as part of their RE curriculum and for acts of worship. In spite of this excellent work, however, the vast majority of our churches only offer their children's ministry on Sunday and the numbers of children attending Sunday services has continued to decline. It has been suggested that nearly half of Anglican churches claim they have no children at all.

The immediate reaction to a statement like that must be to ask whether it is strictly true. It is true that the youngsters who come to church on Sundays are almost entirely the children of the adult congregation. It is true that numbers are often small. If we look beyond Sunday morning, however, we see a more optimistic picture.

There are the children who are worshipping regularly at family services, parent and toddler clubs, midweek activities, and in our Church schools. There are the children who come to Parade services, Mothering Sunday, Harvest Thanksgiving or Christingles. Then there are those who come to school carol services, or as guests at baptisms or weddings and occasionally at funerals.

Then there are the hidden children who use the church hall for sports or drama, who belong to uniformed organizations or visit a church as part of an RE lesson and so on.

Once we go into the community and look at the opportunities, instead of counting the few that come through the church doors every Sunday, our whole perspective changes.

That is what this book is about. It will explore some of the issues concerning today's children and ways in which we, the Church, will have to change our way of thinking and operating if we are to reach them.

USING THIS BOOK

This book can be used in several ways:

- As information and training for clergy or lay people who want to explore the whole subject of evangelism among children.
- To help children's leaders to develop the children's work in their local church.
- Some churches or districts are employing a paid children's worker. Part of his or her brief will include work with non-church children and their families. The material in this book could form part of the basic training.

- Evangelists could use the material to focus on a ministry among children.
- Separate sections can be used as a study guide to developing a particular project, or addressing an issue concerning evangelism among children.

The material is organized in four sections:

- Part One: Children everywhere
- Part Two: Practicalities of evangelism
- Centre point
- Part Three: Opportunities and activities

Part One is designed as a short training course or discussion programme. It could be used by any group of children's workers or church leaders that wants to get to grips with the scenario of today's children and the opportunities and challenges of engaging with them in the community.

It deals with the culture of children and the church's ministry among them at the beginning of the 21st century. It reviews the ways that we can engage with young people but also the obstacles that we unwittingly put in the way of their hearing the Christian story. This provides vital information before exploring any way of engaging with children whether inside or outside the Church family.

Each chapter has a biblical link and, to aid your study, a case study with pointers for discussion or reflection.

Part Two attempts to tell you all the things that you need to know about strategic planning and ways of managing the changes that will happen when you focus on reaching out to children. It includes information on training and ways of getting financial help as well as outlining the legal requirements and support that is available. Many churches do not realize that help is at hand or think that it only applies to large projects, so just reading this may save you money for a start! All the information is earthed in a Bible link and points for reflection and action.

Centre Point, the chapter on worship, could be read in conjunction with any part of this book or on its own. It explores the rationale for our ministry among children—the child's relationship with God. This may involve introducing worship to children who have little or no experience of it. It includes ways of providing a sacred space for God within a busy activity and within the child him/herself. It also provides information on ways of praying that relate to the culture of today's children and imaginative use of music and visual aids.

Part Three begins by reviewing three areas of potential growth—small groups of children, toddlers, and work with local schools. Then it provides advice on running specific clubs or activities. As many of the principles of running one kind of activity are common to all, each chapter should be read in conjunction with Part Two and the Centre Point in order to avoid repeating almost identical material in each chapter.

As with the other two parts, each chapter has a Bible link and pointers for reflection.

The **Postscript** looks forward to your next steps in evangelism among children, the disappointments and the hopes.

READING THIS BOOK

You may be reading this book because you have a particular project in mind or because your church council has asked you to research it. Keep written notes so that when you need to put your plans in action or report to your church leaders or fellow workers you are well prepared.

If you are working in a group, you may find it contains people who have different experiences and perceptions from your own. Concentrate on listening and then contributing to what they have said. We can always learn from each other's experience.

The term 'evangelism' can produce strong feelings and negative views. This is usually from people who have a stereotyped view of it.

A few methods are insensitive and inappropriate, but every situation is different and there are numerous ways of approaching this subject. Do not be afraid to contribute your own experience and thoughts. There is a section about this in Chapter 2, 'Back to where we started'.

Many Christians look at their ministry as operating only from the Church context. You will gain a fuller picture and a lot of first-hand experience if you discuss your ideas with a teacher, club leader or someone with experience of working among children in the community, as well as with people at your church.

However you are exploring this subject, allow God to become part of the thinking and discussion. He longs for children to hear and recognize his voice, so he is the most important companion as you seek to make him known to his children.

NOTE

1. *All God's Children?* GS988 (1991)

PART ONE

CHILDREN EVERYWHERE

Chapter 1

BEING A CHILD TODAY

The last 20 years have seen more changes in a child's life than at any other time in history. The world has been through the fastest technical revolution in the life of this planet, with accompanying changes in lifestyle and economics. This has had a major effect on every single person, but children have been influenced the most.

It would take several volumes to discuss the many factors that have directly or indirectly affected children or the way that we regard them. Instead, let us examine a few things that shape our children's lives, the opportunities and pressures on them and the spiritual journeys that they are undertaking. This will help us to understand them as people in their own right and to highlight the challenges and opportunities that they present to us, the Church.

LAW AND ORDER

Legislation concerning the care and education of children has transformed the ways that children are cared for and the ways that they are expected to learn. The Children Act (1989), the biggest piece of legislation concerning children for over a century, has made the welfare of the child paramount whether in the home, school or the wider community. Health and safety and child protection legislation and guidelines have had enormous effects on voluntary agencies, including the Church. They have forced church councils to take responsibility for their children, and many have risen to the challenge by providing higher standards of care and more training for children's leaders.

The government's policy of *Wrap Around Childcare* (1998) has presented the Church with opportunities for outreach to children in the community through pre-schools, holiday clubs, after-school and even breakfast clubs. The *Sure Start* (2003) plan of a centre in every area geared towards children of less than five years presents yet more prospects for ways in which the local church can be of service.

The Disability Discrimination Act (1995) gives everyone equal access to all services, including voluntary organizations. This has enormous training implications for voluntary bodies that work with children. Churches should always have welcomed children with special needs or disabilities as fellow members of the body of Christ. Now they are legally obliged to do so and to make equal provision for them.

Legislation and schools

Since the National Curriculum was established in 1989, followed by Ofsted inspections, there have been enormous changes in the ways that children are taught and expected to learn. The emphasis at the time of writing is on testing rather than assessment. Many teachers and children have responded well to the challenges, but creative subjects like music and drama are being squeezed out and lack of time and space to play may be a factor in some of the increased behavioural difficulties in quite young children. These are challenges to which the Church could respond through its work among children.

Changes in RE have presented opportunities for children to visit local churches as part of their studies and take part in acts of worship, including the Eucharist. Spiritual development is now officially recognized as an intrinsic part of a child's formation and forms part of Ofsted inspections.

VARIED LIFESTYLES

Family life has altered beyond recognition during the last 20 years. The increase in flexible working patterns has allowed mothers with young children to continue working and put pressure on lone parents to support themselves. Development of 24-hour call centres, Sunday trading, and the explosion of fast food outlets are obvious examples of the changed pattern of work and lifestyle. The services provided are widely welcomed in that they have created jobs and supported busy families but they have reduced the time that some of the poorest parents and children can spend together. The basic structure of daily life has been severely damaged. Shared meals, regular working hours, and Sunday as a day of rest and recreation are things of the past. A large number of children spend some weekends and holiday time with their second parent and often a second family.

Given those trends, it is unrealistic for the church to confine its ministry among children to Sunday morning. It is more sensible to respond to the present social situation by providing holiday, midweek and even breakfast clubs.

POVERTY

The gap between the richest and poorest families has grown. This is not confined to certain regions; neither can affluence be hidden from any part of society. Children have alluring clothes, toys, interests and relationships pumped into their homes through television and computers and see them enjoyed by some of their peers. If, however, they are victims of long-term unemployment, poor housing and the poverty associated with such deprivation, they soon become acutely aware that they lack many of the good things that are enjoyed by other children, maybe even those in the same class at school. These youngsters and their parents need the support of the local church in giving them a place of welcome where they are valued as individuals and given a sense of self-worth.

ICT AND ALL THAT

These changes have had major effects on children's lives. As if that were not enough, there are the rapid developments in technology and children's access to it. In 1990, computers were simple and largely confined to the workplace. The Internet was virtually unknown. Today, nearly half of homes have a PC and every child has access to a computer to study information and communication technology (ICT) at school. Information for homework can be accessed through the Internet quickly and easily. Children play computer games and go to computer clubs. Media reports claim that 75 per cent of children have mobile phones and are more adept than adults at text messaging. The four channels on television have grown literally tenfold, with added entertainment through videos and DVDs.

If this is the average child's way of communicating, we need to provide our children with attractive versions of the Bible, stories that relate to their lives and make the most of the opportunities provided by the Internet.

MULTI-TASK LIVES

The days of 9-to-5 work, a job for life, and a set structure for education are long gone. Flexible working patterns are the norm. Although the curriculum and testing in school are more structured than 20 years ago, there is greater understanding about how children and young people learn. They tend to work in groups or individually. Public exams are a combination of course work and testing. Subjects like music, art and drama stress individual creativity. A wealth of courses is available to people of all ages and lifestyles.

Children talk to friends or text them on mobile phones while walking down the street, having another conversation, or in a club or shop. They can contact people all over the world through the Internet, and play games as well as having conversations while eating a meal or doing another task.

A church service or children's nurture programme with a leader at the front and everyone sitting still and responding together can be quite alien to a child's experience. Indeed, it is more akin to a 'spectator sport' than daily life in school or at home. This does not deny the benefits of corporate worship by a gathered community of all ages, but suggests that flexible prayer activities could be used as well with groups of young people. This is discussed in detail in the Centre Point, 'Worship: making God real'.

SPIRITUALITY AND FAITH DEVELOPMENT

The world at large has a deep interest in spirituality, but this is rarely linked to Christianity. Church is seen to be irrelevant to today's world and even contrary to the principles that it claims to uphold. Most young parents are unfamiliar with church, worship, basic Christian prayers and hymns, yet they claim to have a certain belief and many pray regularly.

Children have a natural spirituality and sense of awe and wonder. This being so, every child whose life you touch will have had some spiritual experience and will have started on a spiritual journey that will last his or her whole life. Our ministry with children and the parents that we meet is to travel alongside them and act as guides and friends. This involves respecting their past experiences, their joys and sorrows as well as proclaiming the good news in a way that is appropriate for them.

Young children have a powerful sense of the nearness but otherness of God. They are susceptible to atmosphere, and experience a sense of his presence in worship and prayer. Some of them will show profound understanding about the nature of God and the way that he works in their lives. God can and does work through children, and the Church that takes this seriously will always be humbled but given a sense of vitality by their perceptions and their ministry.

Gaining confidence

As children develop, they begin to question much of what they have experienced and ask searching questions about faith and life. Most of them would be unwilling to admit to any relationship with God (by any name) or prayer life to their peers. It is not 'cool' to be a Christian and it is very lonely in the playground for the youngster who is open about his or her faith. These youngsters need support from their families, teachers and local church groups if they are to have confidence in their beliefs and the security to explore them.

Although we may go to great lengths to welcome young people as part of the church family, we need to be conscious that they are generally reluctant to belong to any institution, and that this spreads far beyond religious allegiance. For example, many young people do not vote in elections or join societies or clubs. They do, however, have a deep interest in spirituality which is commonly manifested in the idea of God being present within them and a sense of some sort of life after death. This whole subject is explored in Chapter 3, 'Engagement and faith sharing'.

The recent interest in and development of Islam in the West may well lead to a more positive attitude to proclaiming our own Christian faith. In areas and schools with both Christian and Muslim children, the theological perspective is heightened, leading to questions and discussion. This should encourage Christian children to have a more confident and robust attitude to the way that they practise their faith, while respecting their friends of other faiths and cultures.

TIME FOR REFLECTION

Call to mind the children you know and their families. Perhaps they are your own children or close relations. Maybe you work with children or some live near you.

- How do your relations and friends with children organize their meals and free time?
- How many of them work at the weekends or on shifts?
- Do the children have computers at home? Do they use mobile phones?
- What are the things that interest the children you know?
- What can today's children do and enjoy that you could not?

Compare this with the lifestyle of your family and friends when you were a child. This is not about whether one lifestyle was 'better' but appreciating how they are different.

BIBLE LINK

1 SAMUEL 3:1–10

This story about Samuel is of a child hearing and responding to God's call. At first, he thinks it is the voice of his teacher, Eli. It takes time and Eli's guidance before Samuel recognizes God's voice.

Samuel served the Lord by helping Eli the priest, who was by that time almost blind. In those days, the Lord hardly ever spoke directly to people, and he did not appear to them in dreams very often. But one night, Eli was asleep in his room, and Samuel was sleeping on a mat near the sacred chest in the Lord's house. They had not been asleep very long when the Lord called out Samuel's name.

'Here I am!' Samuel answered. Then he ran to Eli and said, 'What do you want?'

'I didn't call you,' Eli answered. 'Go back to bed.'

Samuel went back.

Again the Lord called out Samuel's name. Samuel got up and went to Eli. 'Here I am,' he said. 'What do you want?'

Eli told him, 'Son, I didn't call you. Go back to sleep.'

The Lord had not spoken to Samuel before, and Samuel did not recognize the voice. When the Lord called out his name for the third time, Samuel went to Eli again and said, 'Here I am. What do you want?'

Eli finally realized that it was the Lord who was speaking to Samuel. So he said, 'Go back and lie down! If someone speaks to you again, answer, "I am listening, Lord. What do you want me to do?"'

Once again, Samuel went back and lay down.

The Lord then stood beside Samuel and called out as he had before, 'Samuel! Samuel!'

'I am listening,' Samuel answered. 'What do you want me to do?'

Think or discuss

Faith arises from hearing God speaking our name, discerning it, and then responding to it. For most of us, it will not be a literal call and, as with Samuel, it may be difficult to discern whether it is really the voice of God. We can confuse God's voice with our own wishes or pressures and expectations from other people. Children have enormous pressures from their culture, peer pressure and educational attainment that can cause confusion when they have to make decisions, including recognizing the voice of God.

- Do we believe that God can and does speak to and through children?
- What is the local church's role in being mentors to children as Eli was to Samuel?
- How can we be mentors to children in our Christian community as Eli was to Samuel, so that they develop spiritually and grow in faith?
- How can we help children in our wider community to have an opportunity to recognize and be equipped to respond to God's voice when he speaks their name?
- God's message to Samuel was not a pleasant one, especially for Eli: read verses 11–18. Are we prepared to accept that if we seek to

engage with children on their journey of faith, this will involve change in our church community that some people may find difficult?

CASE STUDY: THE KOS CLUB

The following story is about a church where the children's ministry was tiny. Then the vicar realized that Sunday might not be the best day for the children, and that formal teaching might not be appealing to today's youngsters.

Very few children used to attend St Edward's church, Cheddleton. Numbers fluctuated and, even on a good Sunday, only about six youngsters would turn up for Junior Church.

That was until the vicar, Martin, had the idea of starting Cheddleton's KOS (Kids on Saturdays) club to replace the Junior Church.

Once a month, on Saturday morning, about 35 children meet to play games, have Christian teaching and, of course, enjoy having refreshments and meeting their friends. The club has been running for a year and the children attend regularly. They are led by Pat, one of the clergy and a former infants' teacher, with a team of eight adults, while other members of the congregation help with refreshments. Everyone is very enthusiastic about the project and confidence is growing rapidly.

The children are encouraged to attend and take part in the Family Service the following day. They come from both Methodist and Anglican backgrounds but the majority of the children had no links with a church before they started attending KOS. The Anglican church gears its service towards children of less than ten years, while the older children go on to Crusaders at the Methodist church after that.

Think or discuss

- How was the adult congregation affected by these changes?
- What extra work and cost were caused by these changes?
- How did the children who attended the Anglican and Methodist churches benefit?
- What was the evangelistic perspective of the change in the children's ministry?
- What difference did the KOS club make to the wider community?
- How did the whole worshipping community benefit?

Cost and courage

The financial cost of establishing the KOS club was probably very small but it took courage and ingenuity. It engaged with children and their lifestyles, and the results had a ripple effect on the worship of two churches as well as enabling more youngsters to hear and respond to the Christian story.

Reviewing the way that the Church has engaged with children in the community in the past as well as the present, and discussing the ways that we can meet and share our faith with them, are essential parts of our evangelistic task. They are the subjects of the next two chapters.

Chapter 2

BACK TO WHERE WE STARTED

In this chapter, we review the ways in which the Church has passed on the Christian faith to non-church children for over 200 years. We see how today's society has similar issues to those that challenged the original Sunday School teachers, and how the key aim of their ministry has been allowed to lapse. We also examine the qualities that are needed by those who have a ministry for evangelism among children.

WHAT DO WE MEAN BY 'EVANGELISM'?

The word 'evangelism' is used in this book in the widest sense. It is about witness by presence as much as about teaching and faith sharing. It is about being Christ in the playground or local sports club or pre-school as much as in church-led activities. It involves working with the community by being part of local initiatives and organizations. Most of all, it is about meeting children where they are in every sense and acknowledging their spirituality and experiences of life.

Evangelism among children takes many forms, not least by children among themselves. However it is undertaken, it is about opening doors to the life that Jesus promised, in all its fullness. It is about creating opportunities so that when God puts his hand on a child's shoulder and calls his or her name, as he did to the boy Samuel, that child will be able to recognize his voice and will know how to respond to it.

Patterns of evangelism vary according to the age, situation and culture of the people. They also change according to the way that each generation has understood the great commission to preach the gospel throughout the world (Matthew 28:19–20). We can proclaim the gospel effectively only from within a culture, not from outside it. Our task is not to expect today's children to become like children of the past or to embrace the culture of today's middle-aged church, but to be themselves. This involves our walking alongside them on a pilgrimage that will be a journey of discovery for all of us.

The purpose of this book, therefore, is to help us to find ways of engaging with children in today's culture rather than discussing the relative merits of different evangelistic methods. Before we start, however, it is worth reviewing and learning from the way that children have been taught the Christian faith in the recent past.

'TO READ AND KEEP THE SABBATH'

It is widely assumed that children have always been taught the Christian faith through going to Sunday School. On the contrary, Sunday Schools have existed for only two centuries and were for children who did not attend church. They sprang out of the Industrial Revolution when children were employed for long hours in the factories and mills. Their only free time was on Sunday, when they ran wild in the streets.

Robert Raikes opened the first well-known Sunday School in 1780 in the Sooty Alley area of Gloucester. He was convinced that the underlying cause of crime was ignorance, so he started a school to teach the children from the local factories to read the Bible and to learn basic moral values and behaviour.

Education for all

Similar classes sprang up all over the country. Some attempted to expand the children's education by teaching writing and arithmetic.

The work grew and, whatever the original aims of these pioneers, the principle of free education for all sprang from these roots. Some Sunday Schools became evening classes for adults. Others eventually became day schools; indeed, many of our oldest Church primary schools started life in this way.

A major evangelistic movement

Sunday Schools were probably the biggest evangelistic movement in this country since the time of the Reformation. As free education for all became law, the Sunday School teachers turned their attention to providing basic Christian nurture for children whose parents did not come to church. Millions of children learned Bible stories, the Lord's Prayer and well-known hymns. Memorizing the Ten Commandments, the weekly biblical text and Sunday Collect were commonplace activities. The values and language learned became part of everyday currency.

No system is without its faults, however. Christian nurture followed the educational model, with classes and even examinations, and very little, if any, experience of being part of the worshipping community. The charge that 'adults worshipped God; children learned about him' had more than a grain of truth.

The last 50 years

Changes in the education system at the end of World War II meant that children moved to secondary school at eleven. Sunday School was often rejected at the same time as the youngsters left primary school. Some of them kept contact with the church through youth clubs or uniformed organizations, but far more did not. By the last quarter of the 20th century, with greater mobility and more widely spread families, most non-church parents had stopped sending their children to Sunday School. At the same time, Christian teaching and worship in non-church schools was often of a poor standard and even actively discouraged. Since then, two generations have grown up with little knowledge of the Christian faith or experience of being part of a Christian community.

To nurture Christian children

During the last 20 years, the traditional Sunday School has almost disappeared. It was felt desirable to lose the educational image and to involve children in the worship of the whole Church. Groups became 'Sunday Club' or 'Junior Church', with 'leaders' and a less formal approach. Sessions were held at the same time as the morning service, with the children joining the adults for part of it. That is the most common pattern today. In some churches, the children are welcomed as equal and valued members of the worshipping community. In others, they are a marginalized minority. Most youngsters who attend church on Sunday are the children of the worshipping congregation and the nurture programmes assume a background of Christian knowledge. Numbers are often small and many churches claim that they have no children at all.

Back where we started

In one sense, the Christian nurture of children has come full circle. Flexible working and the demands of a consumerist society leave many families with little time together at weekends, and Sunday as a day of rest and recreation has almost disappeared. Inner cities, urban housing estates and rural areas suffer from deprivation and high unemployment, with children being the most affected. Some parents are simply not available to bring or send their children to church on Sunday morning. For many more families, church attendance is a strange and unfamiliar practice. A large number of children and adults have no knowledge of the Bible or experience of worship, let alone a relationship with a loving God as revealed in Christ.

WHAT ABOUT THE OUTSIDERS?

Attitudes to the place of religion in a child's education, changes in the use of Sunday and the linking of children's nurture to the main Sunday service have combined to leave a huge vacuum in the Church's ministry among children. The majority of churches have little or no outreach to youngsters whose parents do not attend church. Some evangelistic organizations such as CPAS and Crusaders run summer camps for children. Others provide materials and help to churches to organize holiday clubs, fun mornings and midweek clubs geared towards children who have no other links with the church. A more common form of outreach is a monthly Family Service, with visual aids, drama and lively music providing accessible worship for children and the increasing numbers of adults who have little knowledge of the Christian faith. These have been successful in that large numbers of people—usually young families—attend church once a month, but the day and time take no account of the changed use of Sunday in the majority of families.

If we are to reach our children and their parents with the gospel, we need to recover the spirit of those first Sunday School pioneers, by meeting children, engaging with their culture, and responding to their needs. Two hundred years ago, social issues were illiteracy, appalling working conditions, poverty, crime and bad housing with dysfunctional families. Today, they are equally challenging and not very different. The world has changed beyond recognition, but similar issues and needs remain.

✛

TIME FOR REFLECTION

- What are the issues that challenge our society today?
- How are they similar to those at the beginning of the Industrial Revolution when the first Sunday Schools were started?

- Did I go to Sunday School when I was a child? What do I remember about it? Would it be a suitable model for children's nurture today?
- What are the things in today's open-ended week that make Sunday morning a difficult time to get to church?
- Do I recognize that evangelism among children is a journey that adults and children undertake together?
- Do I accept that this journey may change my perceptions as much as those of the children whom I attempt to guide?

BIBLE LINK

2 TIMOTHY 2:1–7

A large part of this book is about specific aspects of our evangelistic work and ways in which the Church can use opportunities to reach children with the Christian story but, before we go further, let us consider what we need to be rather than what we could do.

Timothy, my child, Christ Jesus is kind, and you must let him make you strong. You have often heard me teach. Now I want you to tell these same things to followers who can be trusted to tell others.

As a good soldier of Christ Jesus you must endure your share of suffering. Soldiers on duty don't work at outside jobs. They try only to please their commanding officer. No one wins an athletic contest without obeying the rules. And farmers who work hard are the first to eat what grows in their field. If you keep in mind what I have told you, the Lord will help you understand completely.

What makes a good children's evangelist?

Paul's second letter to Timothy consists largely of personal guidance to his young colleague. This passage contains practical advice for teaching the good news of Jesus to others. He instructs Timothy to pass on his teaching to reliable people so that they in their turn can teach others. This says much about those who teach children or who train children's leaders and seek to evangelize the many children who would not otherwise have an opportunity to hear the Christian story.

A children's evangelist is like a soldier on active service. In Paul's day, this involved being in close combat, looking the opposition in the eye. It involves coming close to people, taking calculated risks, being single-minded, obeying the commanding officer and not being distracted by other matters.

A children's evangelist is also like an athlete. He can win only if he obeys the rules. This involves strict training and the highest professional standards.

Lastly, a children's evangelist is like a farmer. He works hard to sow the seeds, which are so small that they are hardly noticed. He has to bear with disappointments and difficulties caused by poor ground and inclement weather. The harvest will take a long time to come, so he must be patient, continuously caring for the soil. He needs the commitment and expertise to recognize the signs of growth and know how to encourage it.

Think or discuss

- Are we single-minded about helping children to hear the gospel?
- Are we prepared for difficulties and failure?
- Is our work professional or are we content with providing the second-rate?
- Have we proper training and resources?
- Are we aware that evangelism requires patience, or are we expecting quick and maybe superficial results?
- Do we keep in mind that the harvest will come in God's time and place, not ours?

Most of these questions are about attitudes of mind in us and in the church leaders. Changing ways of thinking requires persistence and determination. Some of the requirements, however, can be solved.

Ensuring that children's evangelists have appropriate resources, training and prayerful support is vital. High standards of care and safety are equally important. Most of all, we have to remain true to the gospel and our calling to proclaim it to every generation.

CASE STUDY: GOD'S TIME

Joseph came to England from the West Indies as a young man. The change of culture and the hard life experienced by many immigrants caused him to move away from the Christian faith in which he had been brought up. Many years later, he had a chance conversation with the local vicar in a pub. The conversations continued over a pint on many evenings as they told each other their life stories. In 1994, Joseph was baptized and confirmed. 'It has been a long time,' he said, 'but today is God's time.' Joseph was 84.

Think or discuss

- When were the seeds of Joseph's faith probably sown?
- What can we learn from the way in which Joseph returned to the Christian faith?
- 'It has been a long time, but today is God's time.' What are your thoughts about the years spent between Joseph's arrival in England and his eventual baptism?
- What does this say to us about our relationship with the children whose lives we touch?

Be patient

The journey to faith is a long one, and we live in an age that demands instant results. Some researchers suggest that the time between first enquiring to coming to faith is at least four years. It is hardly surprising that many children's workers get tired after about two and feel that they are getting nowhere!

It is unlikely that activities like holiday clubs will gain many regular church members but giving children an experience of worship and the love of God is a treasure beyond price. It may lead to involvement in Family Services or Christian commitment in later years. We are sowing seeds of faith, and we can trust that, in God's own time, there will be a harvest.

Chapter 3

ENGAGEMENT AND FAITH SHARING

During the last ten years, there has been a large increase in midweek activities offered to children by community projects, schools and churches. A number of churches have found new ways of reaching children from outside the church family at the same time as serving the community. Holiday clubs and fun days are popular, a few churches run breakfast or after-school clubs, and there is an increased focus on work with young children and their parents. Some parishes have a short service in a toddler group or for young families after school or in the early evening. These can be major growth points and, for the parents and children who attend them, the experience of worship and fellowship is indeed 'Church'.

These moves need to be modelled and celebrated. We recall that most of Jesus' ministry was in the streets and the countryside. To confine a ministry with children to an hour a week in a single building that may be inaccessible without a car is not following either his model of teaching or common sense.

FAITH SHARING

The term 'faith sharing' has had nearly as many interpretations as 'evangelism'. At one extreme, it can be little less than coercion. Many years ago, I was confined to a hospital bed, unable to sit up or move much. An elderly lady approached my bedside to give me a lavender bag with a scripture text. She insisted on reading it to me and telling me what it meant to her. There was no opportunity to speak: she finished and departed. The lavender was a delightful gift, but the way of presenting it was intrusive and took no account of my own circumstances or spirituality. How much more beneficial it would have been if we had had a conversation, or even if she had just brought me greetings from her church. I still have the lavender—but I cannot recall the text!

Faith sharing is more about living out of the Christian life than talking about it in a formal setting. A dictionary definition of the word 'share' is 'a portion that a person gives or receives from a common amount'. Sharing puts in as well as taking out.

HOW DOES CHILDREN'S SPIRITUALITY MANIFEST ITSELF?

Children aged up to about seven years have a powerful sense of the presence and wonder of God. They have a vivid imagination and take stories literally. Fairies, witches, invisible friends and, indeed, God, are as real as everyday life.

As they develop mentally, children may start to ask questions about God. Some of these are based on the supposition that God is like a person; others can be deep theological questions: 'What does God look like?' 'Where does he sleep?' 'Why did God let Grandpa die?'

Round about the age of eight, children go through a latent emotional period when they become less spontaneous and affectionate. They start to get their own ideas and make their own decisions. They begin to sort out fact from fiction, and dismiss some of their earlier fantasies and magic. Stories and symbols are still taken literally, so leaders need to be careful when teaching some allegorical stories and abstract concepts like heaven and hell.

As they move towards their teens, children will start to test their faith with questions about the authenticity of scripture, the power of prayer and the problems of pain, hunger and war. We should welcome these discussions and be prepared to give them time and value.

Although God is unchanging, our experience of his presence, style of worship and interpretation of scripture vary according to the age and culture in which we live. Our children have their own spiritual experiences, their own joys and sorrows. Building up of relationships leads to conversations. Waiting for questions and then responding with another question—'What do you think?'—or having a discussion rather than giving a quick answer takes time and patience. The journey of faith is one of searching and wondering that adults and children undertake together and lasts a lifetime.

I WONDER...

Godly Play, a method of learning based on Montessori teaching, seeks to develop natural interests and activities by allowing children to explore a Bible story in their own way and think through their own questions and suppositions in a calm atmosphere. The best opportunities for teaching often come with the throwaway comment from a child or when the children are seated ready to go home, because that is when they ask about things that they really want to know.

Prayer time that allows children to offer their own petitions— maybe just a name or a situation—in a relaxed atmosphere, or to talk informally, allows faith sharing in a far more natural and effective way than formal teaching. This is discussed in detail in the Centre Point, 'Worship: making God real'.

✣

TIME FOR REFLECTION

- Do I acknowledge and respect children's own life journeys?
- Do I believe that children are natural spiritual beings?

- Do I recognize that children have much to give as well as receive?
- Do I allow children time and space to make their own discoveries?

BIBLE LINK

JOHN 4:3–21, 23–26, 28–30

The following passage tells of Jesus' encounter with a woman from another culture and how she comes to faith.

Jesus left Judea and started for Galilee again. This time he had to go through Samaria, and on his way he came to the town of Sychar. It was near the field that Jacob had long ago given to his son Joseph. The well that Jacob had dug was still there, and Jesus sat down beside it because he was tired from travelling. It was midday, and after Jesus' disciples had gone into town to buy some food, a Samaritan woman came to draw water from the well.

Jesus asked her, 'Would you please give me a drink of water?'

'You are a Jew,' she replied, ' and I am a Samaritan woman. How can you ask me for a drink of water when Jews and Samaritans won't have anything to do with each other?'

Jesus answered, 'You don't know what God wants to give you, and you don't know who is asking you for a drink. If you did, you would ask me for the water that gives life.'

'Sir,' the woman said, 'you don't even have a bucket, and the well is deep. Where are you going to get this life-giving water? Our ancestor Jacob dug this well for us, and his family and animals got water from it. Are you greater than Jacob?'

Jesus answered, 'Everyone who drinks this water will get thirsty again. But no one who drinks the water I give will ever be thirsty again. The water I give is like a flowing fountain that gives eternal life.'

The woman replied, 'Sir, please give me a drink of that water! Then I won't get thirsty and have to come to this well again.'

Jesus told her, 'Go and bring your husband.'

The woman answered, 'I don't have a husband.'

'That's right,' Jesus replied, 'you're telling the truth. You don't have a husband. You have already been married five times, and the man you are now living with isn't your husband.'

The woman said, 'Sir, I can see that you are a prophet. My ancestors worshipped on this mountain, but you Jews say Jerusalem is the only place to worship.'

Jesus said to her:

Believe me, the time is coming when you won't worship the Father either on this mountain or in Jerusalem... A time is coming, and it is already here! Even now the true worshippers are being led by the Spirit to worship the Father according to the truth. These are the ones the Father is seeking to worship him. God is Spirit, and those who worship God must be led by the Spirit to worship him according to the truth.

The woman said, 'I know that the Messiah will come. He is the one we call Christ. When he comes, he will explain everything to us.'

'I am that one' Jesus told her, 'and I am speaking to you now.' ...

The woman left her water jar and ran back into town. She said to the people, 'Come and see a man who told me everything I have ever done! Could he be the Messiah?' Everyone in the town went out to see Jesus.

The immediate reaction to this story must be to question what it has to do with reaching today's children. There are, however, many parallels between Jesus' encounter with the woman of Samaria and our meeting children in the community. It is also a vivid example of how Jesus listens to the woman's own cultural and spiritual story. Let us review this passage and see how it can help us to form a model for building our relationships with children.

- Jesus is in a foreign and hostile country. He meets the Samaritan woman on her own territory.
- Jesus asks if she will give him a drink of water. Jews do not have any dealings with Samaritans, and neither would a Jewish man speak to

any woman in public, so he lays himself open to a curt refusal at best and maybe even abuse.

- The woman feels insecure. 'Our ancestor Jacob dug this well for us, and his family and animals got water from it. Are you greater than Jacob?' Later, she says, 'My ancestors worshipped on this mountain, but you Jews say Jerusalem is the only place to worship.' By retreating into the safety of the past, she prevents herself from grasping the opportunities of the present.
- Jesus listens to her and then begins to teach through a dialogue. They challenge each other several times; indeed, the woman 'gives as good as she gets'.
- Then Jesus offers her a way of ending the conversation easily. He says, 'Go and bring your husband.' At this point, the woman could have taken the opportunity to leave him without returning. As it is, she responds to the challenge about her private life and eventually recognizes Jesus as he is. Her reaction is to go and tell others.

What are the implications of this story for the way we reach out to children?

- We have to meet children on their own territory, maybe literally, by going to places where they are—schools, clubs and the street. We should respect their age and culture.
- Attempting to engage with children involves making ourselves vulnerable. We cannot guarantee success; indeed, we may meet rejection or hostility.
- Meeting children where they are involves listening to their stories. This will include finding out about their families, their interests, their hopes and fears. It will mean respecting the spiritual journeys that each one of them will have already undertaken.
- Our teaching should be through dialogue, with each person prepared to listen to and learn from the other. This will include discussion and disagreement at times. It may contain challenges, and adults have to be prepared to be challenged by the child as well as doing some of the challenging themselves.

- Jesus gave the Samaritan woman a 'get-out' clause. One of the most poignant passages in the Gospels must be the story of the rich young man who was anxious to be a disciple. Jesus 'looked closely at him and liked him' but let him go (Mark 10:17–22). If our children do not want to accept what we are offering, we must respect them by letting them leave us with dignity (while holding them in our prayers), not by rejecting them or coercing them to come to church on our terms.
- Coming to faith is about a relationship with God. The Samaritan woman gradually began to recognize Jesus as the Messiah. It may be that a child will come to faith through the way that you imitate Jesus—what you are, not just what you say. This is an awesome responsibility.
- We all know that if children discover something good or exciting, they have to tell others. They may encourage their friends and family to come to faith themselves.

Christian commitment

It is a great privilege to see children growing spiritually as well as mentally and physically as we walk beside them on their Christian journeys. As with other growth, spiritual development can be encouraged through witness and action as well as dialogue, but it has to grow at the pace that the child can manage. We know the dangers of force-feeding and too much cramming of information, as well as those of physical and mental neglect.

We should not aim for, let alone demand, a Christian commitment or formal response from the children we meet. The children have had a good time at a lively holiday club, and asking them, in the emotion and excitement, to 'vote for Jesus' has aspects of heavy-pressure salesmanship. This is not an appropriate way to ask for a lifelong commitment. Most children know the importance of making and keeping promises, and the guilt that arises from finding that they have made a promise they cannot keep will be counter-productive. In the Gospels, Jesus often warns his followers of the cost of 'taking up his cross to follow him'. We should be equally honest with our children and respect their youth and vulnerability.

CASE STUDY: THE CONFIRMATION

Judith's beautiful story helps to illustrate the long-term aspect of engagement and faith sharing with young people. She tells it in her own words.

Sometimes God allows us a glimpse of his bigger picture. One such occasion for me was the confirmation of my godson, 14 years after his baptism. My husband and I had since moved on to two further parishes and this was the first time I had returned to the city centre church where for eight years he had been vicar and I had laboured with under-fives and their families.

Nothing could have prepared me for that evening. I was running late and glad that a seat had been reserved for me in the semi-circular reordered church. It was a good vantage point and I could see most of the congregation and all of the 25 confirmation candidates. One-third of the church was packed with young people. They were relaxed, happy, clearly familiar and comfortable with their surroundings. One-third of the candidates were young people. As I studied their nervous faces, they became strangely familiar. 'Let me help you,' said a voice next to me, and she quickly named the row of fresh-faced teenagers for my benefit. It was like listening to my toddler group register.

At that point, the service began and the church wardens led the bishop from the vestry. Both wardens were mothers who had sat through my first 'enquirers' group. My companion was clearly enjoying the look of surprise and delight on my face and proceeded to recount the members of the PCC and children's leaders' team— numerous parents whose journey with God and the church began in the parent and toddler group. It may have taken some years but it was a humbling moment, which reminded me of 1 Corinthians 3:5–9:

It was the Lord who made it all happen. I planted the seeds, Apollos watered them, but God made them sprout and grow. What matters isn't those who planted or watered, but God who made the plants grow. The one who plants is just as important as the one who waters. And each one will be paid for what they do. Apollos and I work together for God, and you are God's garden and God's building.

Think or discuss

- Judith was privileged to see the results of her labours. Such an experience is gratifying but it is also humbling.
- The young people who had come for confirmation experienced worship and Christian fellowship from a very early age. The welcome and nurture continued. Every child's name was known. Is that the case in your church?
- 'What matters isn't those who planted or watered, but God who made the plants grow.' What does this say about the apparent successes and failures in our efforts to engage with children?

Some children may take the first step of faith because of their contact with you. This step must be recognized and welcomed and helped to grow, maybe leading to baptism or confirmation. We should also remember the story of the labourers in the vineyard (Matthew 20:1–16) and remember that those who volunteered last still received the same reward. The Holy Spirit works in his own way and at his own time.

Chapter 4

MILLSTONES AROUND NECKS

It may seem unnecessary to spend a chapter on the ways in which we, the Church, put obstacles in the way of children hearing the gospel. There may be a temptation to skim through it or to leave it out. Part of our review of children's ministry, however, must be to address any weaknesses or bad practice so that there are firm foundations for new initiatives.

WE DO NOT HAVE ANY CHILDREN!

In P.D. James' novel, *The Children of Men*, she describes a futuristic world in which the increasing sterility among both men and women had come to its logical conclusion. There were no children. It showed that a world without children was not just a world with no future; it was a world without vitality, without freshness and without hope.

It is the same for many of our churches. While there are a few children, they are content to jog along. Once there are none, the worshipping community realizes that it has lost far more than its future generation. Then it acts, but it does not always know how to act. Many clergy lament that they have no children or only very young children in their churches, yet there are children in the streets around them, in schools, sports clubs, health centres and libraries.

What happens on Sunday?

It is very easy to blame outside influences for the lack of children in our churches. We throw up our hands over Sunday trading, boot fairs and sports, and ask how we can compete with such over-powering attractions. However, children stopped attending church, or rather Sunday School, long before any of these activities were invented. If we are honest, we know that if shopping, boot fairs and even computer games were banned on Sundays, it would make very little difference to the number of children attending our churches. Instead of pointing the finger at others, we should ask if there are any obstacles that we, in our own churches, put in the way of allowing children to become part of the worshipping community.

Ministry on Monday

Forget for a moment the common perception that our ministry among children takes place on Sunday and in a church building. Look at it another way. We meet together on Sunday to worship God and meet Jesus through his word and sacrament, but it does not end there. We are the Church, the people of God, being Christ in the community. The Church operates through us for 24 hours a day and seven days each week. Each one of us is a witness to the gospel at every moment. Children (and adults) will learn about what it is to be a Christian by the way we worship God, behave to each other and to the people we meet every day. This is a huge responsibility. Knowing that our behaviour might hinder a child from coming to know Christ is weighty, like a heavy stone.

MEETING CHILDREN WHERE THEY ARE

Jesus' main ministry was in the streets and the countryside. He met people where they were and served their needs. He taught them by telling stories about people they knew, and about familiar things like a child, a mustard seed, and a rare pearl, and they learned something of the nature of the kingdom of God through it. As we have already discussed in Chapter 2, we need to do the same by engaging with children both physically and culturally, instead of expecting them to come to us or to embrace our culture. This includes using language and situations that relate to their lives today, just as Jesus did to his listeners.

A two-pronged approach

If we are to share the gospel with children, we need a two-pronged approach. We must consider the many opportunities for reaching children in the community and decide what strategy to employ. At the same time, we must put our own church in order so that we are ready to welcome children. The benefits of the best holiday club in the world are lost if, having invited children to join you on Sunday, they find that their expectations are not fulfilled, the worship is inappropriate and the nurture is poor.

Unseen and uncounted

The answer to the common lament, 'We have no children in our church' is 'Are you sure?' Contrary to popular opinion, children do come to church, but they are not always noticed or counted. They come to weddings, baptisms and occasionally funerals. They come to the Christingle, Mothering Sunday and Harvest services, and the uniformed organizations come on Remembrance Sunday and the Sunday nearest to St George's day. They use the church for their RE and history lessons. The welcome, quality of worship that they receive and information about the church's activities for children will make them decide whether or not to come again.

An all-age culture

Two centuries of Sunday School has led to an assumption that children are not suitable to worship with adults; indeed, that church services belong to adults. We have forgotten that for centuries, and in some cultures today, the norm has been for people of all ages to worship together. We need to recover the Church as an all-age community where everyone is 'us' and nobody is 'them'.

This means that, although there is a place for a crèche or for children to be nurtured in a way that is appropriate for their age and culture, this should still be seen as a part of the community worshipping together. This entails a major shift in thinking from the concept of children being 'allowed' to come into the adults' service, however welcome they may be made.

✢

TIME FOR REFLECTION

Imagine a typical Sunday in your church and ask yourself the following questions.

- Are children and their families welcomed before they walk through the church doors?
- Is the building warm and pleasant?
- Is there help for families with very young children, such as a crèche area or bags of soft toys?
- Is there a relaxed attitude to the occasional squawk or a toddler heading up the aisle towards the action?
- Is the children's nurture appealing and well resourced?
- Are the children's leaders trained and supported?
- Are children able to join in the services by sitting where they can see, having books, and joining in the hymns?
- Are children allowed to contribute to the worship as readers, intercessors, singers or servers?
- Are children accepted as ministers of Christ with much to give as well as receive?

- Is your church genuinely an all-age community or are some generations marginalized?

Action

If the answer to any of these questions is 'No', stop and think about it seriously. See how you can improve it as a matter of urgency. The best outreach will be unsuccessful if your own church is not already welcoming and affirming its own children and offering worship in which they are fully involved. Some of the questions can be addressed quite easily; a couple may require ingenuity. A few require a change of attitude, and this always takes time. There is further advice on how to address the changes needed in Chapter 8, 'Guiding principles'.

BIBLE LINK

MATTHEW 18:1–6

A country parson once quoted the last sentences of this passage in his parish magazine to encourage his congregation to take its ministry with children seriously. His church warden observed, 'Strong words, Rector. I am not sure I can go along with that', to which the Rector replied, 'You are not criticizing my words. They are the Lord's.'

The disciples came to Jesus and asked him who would be the greatest in the kingdom of heaven. Jesus called a child over and made the child stand near him.

Then he said:

I promise you this. If you don't change and become like a child, you will never get into the kingdom of heaven. But if you are as humble as this child, you are the greatest in the kingdom of heaven. And when you welcome one of these children because of me, you welcome me.

It will be terrible for people who cause even one of my little followers to sin. Those people would be better off thrown into the deepest part of the sea with a heavy stone tied around their necks!

A solemn warning

Jesus' description of the greatest in the kingdom of heaven being like a little child is well known and is usually used to explain the characteristics we need if we are to be part of that kingdom. The sentence about welcoming children, 'when you welcome one of these children because of me, you welcome me', is less frequently discussed. Most of us would rather pass over Jesus' solemn warning, only recorded in Matthew's Gospel: 'It will be terrible for people who cause even one of my little followers to sin. Those people would be better off thrown into the deepest part of the sea with a heavy stone tied around their necks!'

Think or discuss

- Are any of our services geared towards children who have little knowledge of the Christian faith?
- Are we aware of the needs of the children at special services like baptisms? Could we develop them?
- There are seven days in the week. Would it be more appropriate to offer worship and activities geared towards children and their families on a weekday?
- Is the church building always the best venue? Would the school, library, or community centre be a better place to engage with children and their parents through informal worship?
- Do we make the most of the opportunities provided by uniformed organizations and schools visiting the church?

CASE STUDY: ONE PROBLEM, TWO SOLUTIONS

A common pattern in some rural areas is for modern housing to be built on the edge of a village, at some distance from the amenities and the church. The following story is about two ways in which churches responded to similar situations.

St Peter's on the Hill is a medieval church, nearly a mile away from the nearest house. It has no facilities and the congregation is tiny. A new primary school was built about 30 years ago to accommodate the expanding population of young families in the valley. Very few of them had ever been to the church for more than the occasional baptism, so the new minister decided to offer a monthly service after school in a classroom. She arranged ten chairs and hoped for six people. Fourteen came. Six months later, the service had to move into the school hall because the congregation numbered over 50 adults and children, plus several babies.

Lower Sutton is also a medieval village. It remained a small agricultural community until 1980, when a large housing development was built a mile from the church. It turned the rural environment into a town of over 6000 people. The parish church advertised its Sunday School and other activities, which were held in the old village hall. This required a journey across a dual carriageway to the old village and then a walk along a footpath.

A group of new residents decided that they needed a social life for themselves and their children. They started a toddler group at the community centre. The next summer they ran a play scheme in the new school. A five-a-side football club has been established as well as a swap shop for children's clothes. None of the church congregation has any input to these events.

Think or discuss

- What is the main difference in the way the two churches have responded to the challenge of new housing in the parish?

- What do the two situations say about ways of being church?
- Can you think of ways in which links between the congregation worshipping at St Peter's and the 'church in the school' could be developed, or should they be left as they are?
- Having missed opportunities when Lower Sutton was developed, what would be good and bad ways for the local church to engage with the community and its young people today?
- Is there anything that your church can learn from these stories?

During this chapter we have explored the way that Jesus commands us to welcome children and then warns us of the dreadful consequences if we place obstacles in the way of children, and other vulnerable people, coming to him. We have recalled that we are the people of God operating in his world. It is our responsibility to proclaim the gospel to each generation. We need to address the obstacles that make it difficult for children to be part of our worshipping community, and celebrate the many occasions when children are present with us. At the same time, we need to be in that community, engaging with the children we meet there.

The next chapter looks at a few of the opportunities that are provided in the community and ways in which the church and other organizations can work in partnership.

Chapter 5

PARTNERS IN THE COMMUNITY

A vicar arrived in his urban parish. He looked at the facilities offered by the council and local community groups and realized that there was very little for children. His first step was to phone the Mayor and say, 'Let's work together!'

The resulting project drew together church and community leaders, government funding and donations from Christian charities. The results have benefited the whole neighbourhood and the church's ministry among children is flourishing. The same rule applies to a project of any size: it is best to look at the opportunities and help available in the community, and work in partnership when appropriate rather than working in isolation.

CALLED TO BE YEAST AND LIGHT

It is a sad fact that most Christians are bad at working with other people. They are not even very good at working with their fellow Christians in other churches. Yet Jesus called us to be like yeast in flour, or light in darkness. A lump of yeast and a sack of flour are not much use on their own but, made into bread, can feed a whole village. A candle does not have much effect if it is hidden away but, placed strategically, its light can transform a darkened room. In the same way, a Christian can enliven and transform the lives of those who have drab and dull existences.

Exploring your local community

Having spent time looking at children past and present and the way that we should engage with them, we need to put them into context: the community in which they live. If you have lived in the same district or village for several years, you will probably know quite a lot about what is happening locally. This is especially so if you are retired, unemployed or at home with young children. Some people, however, can have lived in the same place for 20 years and still not be aware of the services and activities that are available for children in the area.

Make enquiries from neighbours with children, schools, health visitors and community centres to find how children spend their spare time and what needs they have. Look at the noticeboard in your community centre or village hall, and in your supermarket and newsagent. What is offered for children?

If you receive a newspaper or a contact phone book from your local authority, look in it to find out what is provided in the wider area, and note the names and contact details of any departments that might be useful.

The following is a list of the amenities and clubs for children that you may find in a large village or small town:

- After-school club
- Ballet or tap dancing classes
- Beavers and Rainbows
- Breakfast club
- Brownies and Cubs
- Children's clothes swap shop
- Drama workshop
- Five-a-side football
- Health centre
- Holiday play scheme
- Junior athletics or sports club
- Library

- Music lessons
- Pre-school
- Toddler club
- Toy library

When we add the activities that may be available at school or in a larger town, such as computer clubs, tennis and swimming lessons, the picture is one of very busy children occupied for every waking hour.

This is not so for every child, however. In some areas, there is very little for children, and your church may be in one of those areas. Maybe there are very few children because you live in a small village. Maybe you live in an inner city or on an urban housing estate, where the children have little to do because there is not the money, the resources or the determination to provide more than the bare necessities of life. Your locality may be well resourced but contain families who cannot afford the fees or have difficulty in taking their children to the various activities. This is developed later in the paragraph on neglected areas in Chapter 8, 'Guiding principles'.

How the community can help the church

- Business sponsorship
- Children's charities
- Children's Information Service register (CIS)
- Council grants and sponsored places
- Early Years Development and Child Care
- Health visitor and centre
- Local authority advice and training including:
  - Child development, play-work and so on
  - Child protection
  - First aid
  - Inspection of premises
  - Health and safety
  - Registration of group

- Local people speaking at club nights
- Park and sports ground
- Premises: community centre, library, room in a pub, supermarket
- Publicity: local paper, noticeboards, radio, website
- Resources centre, toy library, loan of equipment
- School
- Sure Start programme

How the church can serve children in the community

- After-school child care or homework club
- Befriending lonely parents
- Breakfast club
- Church building for RE or other lessons
- Church hall or room to let to children's groups
- Dedicated and trained children's workers
- Help in school
- Holiday clubs and play schemes
- Interest groups: bell ringers, choir and so on
- Meeting place for children and estranged parents
- Pre-school
- Saturday clubs
- Special services
- Toddler group or buggy service
- Uniformed organizations

TRUST, TIME AND PATIENCE

The aim of the above lists is to encourage you to see where the community can help you in your outreach among children and where the church in turn can be of service to the community. Do not be daunted by the number of opportunities that are presented.

A simple profile of children and the community

1. Take a wide piece of paper. Divide it into six columns. Head them:
   a) Children's activity
   b) Church-led group
   c) Community group
   d) Church links
   e) No connection
   f) Not happening

2. Write every children's activity you can think of in the first column. If you are in a village, review a larger district, such as the benefice or the area served by the local school. Now make a profile of the way your community provides for its children and the ways that the church contributes to it, by putting ticks in the other five columns as appropriate.

3. Look at the church-led groups you have ticked in column b. Ask if they are going well. If they are not, ask whether they can be improved or have outlived their usefulness and should be discontinued.

4. Look at columns c and d. Note where there are church links with the existing community groups. Maybe they use church premises, or a member of the congregation is a leader or works there. These are all opportunities. Consider whether your church could strengthen links with community groups or organizations.

5. Look at columns c and e. Are there links that you have not noticed? Maybe a member of the congregation is already involved with the community group, through his or her children. That is witness. It may be worth discussing with that person if the church can be of service to the group. If there are no links, discuss whether there is a way in which the church can make an initial contact.

6. Now look at the ticks in the last column. Can you see a place or situation where children are not being catered for, that could be of help? For example, some children may be dropped off very early before school and their families would respond to a breakfast club. There might be young parents who would value a toddler group. There may be Beavers for boys, but not Rainbows for girls. This may be because there is no demand, but it may be because nobody has thought about it or there is nobody to run it. That is for you to find out.

Building bridges

Building up relationships with the wider community and particular organizations means trust on both sides. This takes time and patience. Because Jesus' ministry was in the community, ours must be there too. Helping with children's activities that are already operating can be effective witness and more sensible than starting something new that may not be needed. Always consider working with existing church or community projects before striking out on your own.

We will revisit your profile when reading Chapter 6, 'Aims and audits'.

✛

TIME FOR REFLECTION

You have just assimilated an enormous amount of information. You may have known some of it already. On the other hand, you may not have considered the help that is available, or ways in which Christians can witness by serving in the community.

Pause before moving on to the second part of the book. Most of the information given in this chapter is expanded in future chapters. As preparation, ask yourself the following:

- What is my church doing already? Should the first step forward be to improve it?
- What has immediately appeared useful or particularly interesting to me?
- How could I, or my church, be of more service in the community?

BIBLE LINK

MATTHEW 5:13–16

Sometimes we feel that trying to reach children with the Christian story is like dropping pebbles down a black hole. The task is too big for us to be effective. In this passage from the Sermon on the Mount, Jesus reminds his little band of followers how small things like salt and light can make a huge difference to the world if they are used to full effect.

You are like salt for everyone on earth. But if salt no longer tastes like salt, how can it make food salty? All it is good for is to be thrown out and walked on.

You are like light for the whole world. A city built on top of a hill cannot be hidden, and no one would light a lamp and put it under a clay pot. A lamp is placed on a lampstand, where it can give light to everyone in the house. Make your light shine, so that others will see the good that you do and will praise your Father in heaven.

Think or discuss

- Have we confined our plans for engaging with children to church-led activities?
- Have we realized that Jesus calls us to live in such a way that the interests of our neighbour are served rather than our own?
- Are we aware that being salt and light in the world will involve cooperating and working within the wider community?

CASE STUDY: BUILDING BRIDGES

John Guest is Rector of Stanford-le-Hope, on the Thames Estuary in Essex. His ministry in the local schools over the last decade was a tireless and vibrant one, but he realized that so much more could be done if he had a schools' worker. He describes in his own words how the schools and churches worked together with support from the local community to make this dream come true.

Joining in partnership is always a good thing, and in the sphere of church and schools work this is particularly true. There are ten schools in my parish and I am delighted to say that we are involved in all of them. With such good contact with local schools, it has long been my desire to appoint a schools' worker who could strengthen the links between the schools, the churches and the community. Neither schools nor churches have a particularly good record of working together so it has been great to see them coming together for this particular project, especially as it was initiated by the parish church.

Early discussions with head teachers proved so favourable that I was able to persuade them to make a financial contribution to the project. Nine of the schools promised over one-third of the annual cost of the schools' worker and two other local churches backed the scheme. The rest of the funding came from grants and awards. The project was planned in association with Scripture Union, who are highly experienced in work with schools, and a local Trust, chaired by me, with the local Methodist minister, a house church leader, two primary head teachers, an RC teacher representing the secondary schools and a local mum acting as administrator. Partnership again! It has been amazing how well we have worked together.

The project is now up and running. The schools' worker, Steve, works with each school in a variety of ways from leading worship and taking RE and PSHE lessons to helping with circle time and pastoral support. He also liaises with the church youth worker. He is already providing a much-needed link between the churches and the education system, to the benefit of the wider community. Through our partnership, we have discovered that the bigger the barrier we have to breach, the better the bridge we have built.

Think or discuss

- What did John establish before he started to think about having a schools' worker?
- How were local community projects and people involved?
- What initiative came from the schools?
- What is the strength in the management of the project?
- Although this is a huge project, it started as a grain of salt, a vision. What hope does that give to the evangelism among children by our church?
- Can we use John's project as guidance for our own smaller plans?

Action

You may find that just reading this chapter has fired you. You have suddenly noticed the many opportunities for engaging with children in the community. You have realized that help is available and that this includes training and money. Do not try to cover everything at once. Store the information in your mind, and use it as a background for the next chapter, in which we explore the aims behind an evangelistic strategy among children.

PART TWO

PRACTICALITIES
OF EVANGELISM

Chapter 6

AIMS AND AUDITS

GO TO THE CHILDREN

We have already observed that a common lament from clergy and children's workers is either 'We haven't got any children' or 'We only have three or four children.' Some rural communities have literally only two or three children living in the village. In some inner-city areas, there are only a few young families or the majority of the population is of other faiths. For the most part, however, this is not the case. The speaker means that only a few children come through the church door on Sunday morning, while there may be literally thousands living in that parish.

There are some lovely stories of young people coming into a church out of curiosity on a cold winter's evening, to find a welcome and acceptance, but they are the exception rather than the rule. We have already recognized that the Church needs to go to where the children are and be alongside them if it is to reach them with the good news of the gospel. This needs strategic planning and careful use of our resources if it is to be effective.

WHY ARE WE DOING THIS?

Let us move back a step in order to review why we are trying to reach children in the community. What are our underlying aims? What do we hope will happen?

We may express it in different ways but the underlying aim must be that children will have the life that Jesus promised—life in all its fullness. This is about wholeness, and the implications are huge. They incorporate human rights, theology of childhood, cultural, social and educational issues and basic good practice like health and safety and child protection. Most Christians believe that every child has a right to be a whole person, and that this is most fully expressed when he or she has come to have a relationship with God as revealed through Christ.

Sharing something precious

Strangely, this is rarely the immediate answer to the question 'Why are we trying to reach children?' although it is often expressed after some discussion. The most common reply is that children will come to church, and it can be followed by a comment about ensuring the church's future for the coming generations. That is understandable, especially when it comes from a small and ageing congregation. It wants to share something precious and keep it for posterity. If the questioner probes further and encourages the speakers to say more, they will often make an affirmation of a deep and sustaining faith that they learned as children and a longing for today's children to receive the same.

It takes gentleness and sensitivity to explain that yesterday's methods will not work in today's world, but most older people understand a great deal about patience and disappointment, so will be aware that they may not see any immediate results. Indeed, many older people have a great deal of wisdom and experience, so they are acutely aware of the need for change so that the Church can be active in the community.

Other aims

In some churches, there will be a strong message from a particular theological standpoint in which Jesus' atoning sacrifice on the cross is central, with the need for repentance and conversion, and a choice between good and evil. Other answers will include comments about social need, children not learning about the Bible in school and about the Church serving in the local community.

Before going further, have an open discussion about your aims and objectives. This will clear up any misunderstandings and help people to articulate the value that they put on communicating their own faith.

COMMON AIMS AND OBJECTIVES

The reasons for reaching children will be a mixture of spiritual and social motives:

• Witnessing to the gospel through working with children in the community.
• Helping children and their parents to experience worship in an informal setting.
• Giving children accessible ways of worshipping God and learning Bible stories.
• Helping children to know Jesus as their Saviour and friend.
• Encouraging more children and parents to come to church.
• Providing a service to the local community.
• Supporting young families.

Results may include:

• Children discovering the gospel and worshipping God in a way that is appropriate for their age and culture.
• Children's natural spirituality being given a chance to grow in a Christian context.
• Giving babies an experience of worship from a very early age and parents an opportunity to ask questions and discuss matters concerning their lives and faith.
• Older children experiencing Christian teaching and worship,

which may lead to their attending the Family Service or special services like Christingles.

- Some of the children coming to Christian commitment as adults, or returning to church to be married or have their children baptized.

A ministry among children in the community is not guaranteed to increase the Sunday morning congregation, but a positive and open attitude to any evangelistic work is important. So is the prayerful support of every person in the Christian community.

Our God is a generous God. We are constantly surprised and humbled by his open-handed generosity to us. We may well find that we are blessed and invigorated through our relationship with these children. A church that takes children seriously always receives a sense of vitality and hope through them.

✣

TIME FOR REFLECTION

What do we hope will happen as we reach out to children? Do we have any kind of vision or is it just something that we think that we ought to do?

BIBLE LINK: A STRATEGY

LUKE 10:1–11

This is Luke's account of a strategic walking witness. He does not describe what the disciples taught but goes into detail about the way that they were to act. See how the passage can relate to your outreach.

The Lord chose seventy-two other followers and sent them out two by two to every town and village where he was about to go. He said to them:

A large crop is in the fields, but there are only a few workers. Ask the Lord in charge of the harvest to send out workers to bring it in. Now go, but remember, I am sending you like lambs into a pack of wolves. Don't take along a money bag or a travelling bag or sandals. And don't waste time greeting people on the road. As soon as you enter a house, say, 'God bless this home with peace.' If the people living there are peace-loving, your prayer for peace will bless them. But if they are not peace-loving, your prayer will return to you. Stay with the same family, eating and drinking whatever they give you, because workers are worth what they earn. Don't move around from house to house.

If the people of a town welcome you, eat whatever they offer. Heal their sick and say, 'God's kingdom will soon be here!'

But if the people of a town refuse to welcome you, go out into the street and say, 'We are shaking the dust from our feet as a warning to you. And you can be sure that God's kingdom will soon be here!'

Think or discuss

- Jesus sent the disciples out in pairs so that they could support and bear witness to each other. He enthused them by describing the opportunities but warned them about the dangers and stresses. A ministry with children can be very rewarding but it is hard work.
- Jesus sent them ahead of him to prepare for his teaching. They were to find places where he would be welcomed. Only then would he come to proclaim his good news. Evangelism takes time and patience.
- Jesus gave strict orders about travelling light and about behaviour towards the people the disciples would meet on the way. We need to be single-minded. A few items are essential for our work but trained and committed people are the best resources.
- Jesus gave instructions about the way to respond to being welcomed or shunned. The disciples were to start work and accept

help in the shape of hospitality. We need to learn to accept help and work with other people or organizations besides our fellow Christians.

- If the disciples were rejected, they were not to persist with their message but simply move on to another place. We need to learn to recognize when a project is not going to succeed, then review the situation and approach it from another angle, or even set it aside in favour of another one.

Alongside considering our aims and reflecting on Luke's report of a mission strategy, we need to undertake a simple audit of the local children and their lives in the church and the whole community. Turn to the profile you drew up when you were studying Chapter 5, 'Partners in the community'. Look again at the conclusions you drew from it.

Danger! Overload!

This kind of audit can fill children's leaders with enthusiasm but there is a real danger of willing helpers becoming overloaded. Some households have the ruling that when a new item of furniture or clothing comes into the house, something has to go out. It is the same with the use of time and talents.

Many new projects collapse because the church has not looked at them in the context of its other ministries. Before taking on a new project, ask what will have to be given up to make space for it. It takes courage to close something that has run its course or is failing, but this has to be done if new work is to flourish. Hard pruning produces the strongest growth, whether in a church's programme or a rose bush!

In the Bible link, Jesus told his disciples to move on if they were not going to succeed. Plan carefully and work slowly, but if there is complete apathy or strong opposition, do not hurl yourself at the barricades. Learn from the experience and do something else or try again elsewhere.

Jesus also told his disciples to accept hospitality. Look for people in your community who could help or advise you. Maybe the head teacher in your school would offer premises or advice. So could local Christian workers—for example, a member of BRF's Barnabas ministry team, or a Scripture Union schools' worker, or a Church Army officer. There is a list of help provided by the local council in Chapter 5, 'Partners in the community'.

Make haste slowly

Whatever needs and opportunities for outreach you have noted, do not feel that you personally have to do them or, indeed, that somebody has to address them all. Take one thing at a time, plan it carefully and develop the work slowly. An initial burst of enthusiasm can lead to trying to do too much at once. It inevitably ends with bankruptcy or burnout.

There are two big questions:

• How do we prioritize the opportunities that we have for outreach?
• How do we manage the changes that will occur?

These are the places where new work often falls down, and they are the subject of the next chapter.

Chapter 7

CHANGE AND ACT

OWNING THE WORK; MANAGING THE CHANGE

One of the biggest challenges in developing children's work (or any other work, for that matter) involves persuading the church community to accept and own the resulting changes. Many plans run into problems because the congregation feels that it has not been consulted, and does not know what is happening. Gossip and fear take over, with the inevitable distortion and exaggeration. The feeling of threat bears little relation to the size of the change; individuals may feel just as strongly about providing a shelf in a cupboard for the toddler club as about having major changes to the time and style of worship.

However simple your plans are, if they are to be successful and last beyond a single event, your church community needs to be fully informed about what is happening and the thinking behind it. It gives each person an opportunity to respond and to own the project, even if he or she does not want to be personally involved with it. One of the most common obstacles to evangelistic work among children is that the parish fails to see it as an integral part of its ministry within the wider community.

If any change is to be effective, it needs a framework of careful research, preparation, a shared vision and adequate resources. This applies as much to small events as to major projects.

A FRAMEWORK FOR CHANGE

There are four vital components to any successful change:

- Pressure for change
- A clear, shared vision
- Adequate resources
- A planned programme

Pressure for change

Pressure for change may come from within the church or, indeed, the present children's work, or it could come from the wider community, such as the local school, another church or a group that meets on church premises. A lot of children's work fails because there is no determined force to keep it on the agenda.

A clear, shared vision

A clear, shared vision is necessary if the idea is to be sustained. The most wonderful holiday club or exciting service will not be repeated, let alone developed, if the church council and the congregation show no interest or do not understand the reasons why this particular activity is happening. Information and prayerful support are essential.

Adequate resources

Any activity has to be properly resourced. It is a case of 'cutting one's coat according to one's cloth'. If the same people are leading a group week after week with inadequate help, if there is a shortage of basic equipment or you have to fund-raise to pay the bills, the result will be anxiety and frustration. Start where you are, not where you want to be, and work within your limits regarding number of people, facilities and budget. As we have already discussed, be prepared to cut back on work that is unsuccessful or no longer needed.

A planned programme

Planning is vital. If the first steps are not planned properly, the project will be disorganized, with false starts as the leaders try to make policy or correct mistakes as they go. Meanwhile the children will be dissatisfied and may not give you another chance. They do not have voices and, if their needs are not recognized, they will simply vote with their feet.

The following chart may be of help:

Pressure for change	+	Shared vision	+	Adequate resources	+	Planned first steps	=	Change
	+	Shared vision	+	Adequate resources	+	Planned first steps	=	Bottom of heap
Pressure for change	+		+	Adequate resources	+	Planned first steps	=	Fast start that fizzles
Pressure for change	+	Shared vision	+		+	Planned first steps	=	Anxiety and frustration
Pressure for change	+	Shared vision	+	Adequate resources	+		=	Haphazard; may collapse

✝

TIME FOR REFLECTION

Think about any change that has occurred at your place of work or your church or in your family life recently. It may be something quite small that would affect a lot of people, like using a new hymn book, or something huge, like moving house. Measure it against the four headings in the chart.

- Did the change have all these components?
- Was it totally successful?
- Where were there problems? Were they caused by the lack of one of these components?

BIBLE LINK

ACTS 6:1–6

Large parts of Luke's writing are about practical action or how issues are addressed in the early Church. The story of the seven helpers is one of them.

A lot of people were now becoming followers of the Lord. But some of the ones who spoke Greek started complaining about the ones who spoke Aramaic. They complained that the Greek-speaking widows were not given their share when the food supplies were handed out each day.

The twelve apostles called the whole group of followers together and said, 'We should not give up preaching God's message in order to serve at tables. My friends, choose seven men who are respected and wise and filled with God's Spirit. We will put them in charge of these things. We can spend our time praying and serving God by preaching.'

This suggestion pleased everyone, and they began by choosing Stephen. He had great faith and was filled by the Holy Spirit. Then they chose Philip, Prochorus, Nicanor, Timon, Parmenas, and also Nicolaus, who worshipped with the Jewish people in Antioch. These men were brought to the apostles. Then the apostles prayed and placed their hands on the men to show that they had been chosen to do this work.

So the early Church was not always as idyllic as the early chapters of Acts suggests. In fact, it was rather like it is today! The widows from the Hellenic synagogues were complaining that they are being neglected in favour of the local Aramaic-speaking widows. The Greek speakers were immigrants who had settled in Jerusalem. It is easy to imagine why these widowed immigrants faced special hardship and that their needs might be ignored when the local leaders distributed food.

Luke records the procedure for addressing the problem in detail. There is a desire to address the problem. The whole community is involved in selecting the seven 'deacons'. They are given a clear brief and resourced by being commissioned by the apostles and the support of the whole community. Note that the apostles do not try to take on the extra work but delegate it to new people.

Think or discuss

- How can we model this pattern as we develop our work with another marginalized group, the children who are not part of our worshipping community?
- Do we pray for our children's workers and publicly affirm their ministry?
- Are Church leaders prepared to delegate their authority and are we prepared to receive it?
- If we intend to start new work, what should we stop doing?

GROWTH

You may find that you do all of the right things, yet somehow it does not work. No person or method can guarantee success or growth. As we read in Chapter 2, 'Back to where we started', a children's evangelist has to be like a farmer. He sows the seeds, which are so small that they are hardly noticed. He has to create the environment and conditions that encourage growth. This is a long-term job if the ground has been neglected, and he will have to bear with disappointments and difficulties. He uses the best resources that he has to ensure growth and knows that it cannot be forced or hurried. God is the true evangelist and, in his kingdom, increase and the ensuing harvest belong to him and not to us.

Chapter 8

GUIDING PRINCIPLES

Having reviewed the children, their world, what we mean by evangelism and the ways that we, the Church, can engage with children, the next two chapters focus on the framework of an evangelistic project and the resources available to support it.

Always keep in mind the four criteria for success in any major project:

- Pressure for change
- Clear, shared vision
- Adequate resources
- Planned programme

RESEARCH

Before presenting any ideas to a church council or starting initial planning, you need to decide what sort of activities are needed and what facilities you will need to provide for its successful operation. If it is an entirely new venture, start with a single event like a fun morning or a toddlers' tea party, even if your sights are set on a regular club. Only consider a long-term project when you have organized several short events and know that you have experienced helpers who are used to working together.

Explore the community

Ask questions in your local community as well as at your church. Discover what activities and clubs for children already exist. The best way to do this is by drawing up a profile of your parish or locality as described in Chapter 5, 'Partners in the community'. Always seek to co-operate with and complement other organizations.

• Offer to help with an existing organization that is short of leaders rather than starting a new one.
• Look for a free afternoon rather than competing with other clubs and activities.
• If another church holds a holiday club or there is a local authority play scheme, consider offering to help with it, or hold yours on another week with a different programme.
• If there is a social need that is not being filled, talk to your local authority and see if you can work together to address it.

Neglected areas

Discover whether there is an area where nobody has any connection with your church. Maybe it is not easily accessible, on the far side of the railway line or an estate with high-rise flats. Many new housing developments are remote from the centre of the community and have few facilities. It could be that some of your present children's work could be replicated in a new location or that you should start new work or worship there rather than at the church building.

Rural areas

If you are in a village, any activity will belong to the whole community whether the church leads it or not. Consider where the majority of the children live, where the facilities are and what transport is available so that the children can meet in a single place.

Consider whether providing a mini-bus to bring people to a monthly service or children to a holiday club would be possible.

Place and people

Having decided where there is a need to which you can respond, think about where you will hold your club and who will help to run it. The kind of club that you can hold depends on the numbers of leaders available, the size of the premises and standard of facilities. The Children Act and health and safety legislation help to ensure that our children's activities take place in safe and well-maintained premises with adequate numbers of adults present. Once you have your venue and basic team of adults settled, then you can decide how many children you can involve and what the programme will be.

VENUES

The church hall

The church hall is the most obvious choice for a children's club. It is familiar, cheap and it makes it easy to form links with other church activities. Some activities or worship can take place in the church building. Check that it fulfils basic safety standards and is suitable for young children. Your local Social Services will usually inspect premises and advise on the number and age of children that would be appropriate. If you rent your hall to groups that include children, this will probably have been done already.

Before choosing the hall, consider whether or not it is easy to reach from the children's homes and schools, or if there is a more accessible option.

If your church is considering refurbishing or developing its hall or building a church room, see that plans include provision for young children as well as adults.

The church

The church is the only available building in some communities. The disadvantages of holding a children's club in an ancient building are obvious, but with good heating and lighting, plus some imagination, quite a lot can be achieved. If the church has chairs, they can be moved to create an open space. A corner of the church or space under the tower could be made into a children's corner for prayer and worship but also for meetings of a small toddler group. The churchyard is a wonderful area for nature trails and treasure hunts. Much can be taught about the Christian faith by exploring the church building. The advantage of using the church building is that the children will get to know it in an informal situation and then will be at ease if they visit it for a main service.

Schools

Schools are designed for children and have resources ranging from play space to suitable furniture and toilets. Children are familiar with them. An after-school club would be a natural continuation of the school day. It might be possible to run a club during the lunch hour. If you use a school, it is important to remember that you are a guest and should respect the layout of classrooms and refrain from using school equipment without specific permission. You will almost certainly have to pay rent for the premises and will have to remove all equipment at the end of each session. That, however, would be balanced by the convenience of having purpose-built premises and could be a valuable way for the church and its local school to work together.

Public places

Village halls and community centres are the obvious meeting place for any public event. Churches have run children's clubs in libraries, rooms in pubs and even doctors' waiting rooms. Some supermarkets have invited churches to run Christian clubs for children while parents do the shopping. They will all have basic facilities and may even be free of charge. These options should be actively considered rather than being a last resort. Being there will witness to the community and reach people who would normally not attend a church service.

HALLMARKS OF SUCCESS

Having fulfilled the conditions for managing the change, let us turn to the activity itself. There is no perfect success story, for every situation is different. There are, however, a few criteria that are common to most good children's work.

1. Vision

Most successes start through the vision of a few people. They see a need and address it. That vision needs to be shared and owned by the church community.

2. Pastoral care

We read in the Bible link in Chapter 7 of the importance of pastoral care and personal contact with marginalized people. Children need to be known and valued. This involves taking an interest in their lives, getting to know their families and visiting them regularly. In other words, it is hard work!

3. Service

Part of engaging with children may include responding to social need by serving the community. This is part of our Christian witness and is of the highest value. It has to be properly led and resourced.

4. Appropriate engagement

Effective children's work will engage with the children where they are, in every sense. The level of Christian witness, teaching and worship should be that which is appropriate for the situation and should be planned as carefully as any other aspect of the activity.

CLUBS AND ACTIVITIES

Let's spend some time reviewing the most common ways that the church engages with children. They are discussed in detail in Chapters 11—16.

1. The local school

The local school provides the greatest opportunity for a church to engage with children. Even the smallest of village schools will have representatives of up to a hundred families of all ages and backgrounds, meeting together every day—children, teachers, classroom assistants, mid-day meals supervisors, cleaners, parents and governors. Every church should give priority to utilizing the many opportunities that exist for a creative relationship with this group of people of all ages and backgrounds.

2. Pre-schools and toddler clubs

Pre-schools and toddler clubs meet regularly in church halls. Some of them are church-led; other groups are there as tenants. They provide opportunities for contact with the parents and youngsters. A monthly act of worship with songs, simple prayers and a short talk gives children an opportunity to experience worship from an early age. It also allows the parents to worship and enquire about their faith in a relaxed environment.

3. Fun mornings or holiday clubs

Fun mornings or holiday clubs are the most common way for churches to provide Christian teaching in a 'fun' environment. Some are followed by a special service on the next Sunday. Others contain basic Christian teaching, designed for children with little knowledge of the Christian faith. For many churches, the annual holiday club is the biggest and most successful form of outreach.

4. Saturday morning clubs

Saturday morning clubs are usually held once a month or as single events. Some of them are preparation for a special service on the following day. Others provide a safe environment for children while their parents are shopping. In rural parishes where there are too few children or amenities to provide nurture in their own churches, they may be organized ecumenically or across a deanery in place of the traditional Sunday meeting.

5. Breakfast clubs

Breakfast clubs are a new and fast-growing culture. Most operate in schools, so that the family can eat together and then the children are cared for while the parents continue with their journey. A few churches are offering a similar service, with the children being escorted to school by church members.

6. After-school clubs

After-school clubs have operated in the community for a decade. Most of them are held in schools or community centres. Some of them are homework or latchkey clubs; others are geared to a particular interest—for example, sport or music. The number of clubs is growing but demand far outstrips supply. An increasing number of churches see such a club as a major form of outreach.

7. Uniformed organizations

Uniformed organizations do valuable work with children and young people. Some have formal links with a church, but many other groups will attend the local church on Remembrance Sunday or for a St George's day parade. These small links provide many opportunities that need to be valued and encouraged.

8. Special interest clubs

Clubs with a particular focus—sports, drama, music and so on— provide a valuable service to the children in the community. Helping with one of these activities may not seem to be obvious evangelism but, as we have already established, witness is as important as more overt outreach.

9. Church activities

Singing in a choir, bell ringing or serving are still ways through which children take the first steps of faith. Children who do not normally attend church but enjoy music often join children's choirs or music groups. We must never forget that the faith is caught as well as taught, and that children, through taking part in beautiful liturgy, may receive a sense of the presence of God that will last them for the rest of their lives.

LEADERS AND HELPERS

It is usually better to seek out and invite people to help with children's work than to wait for volunteers. Some people are reluctant to volunteer because they wonder if they have the skills needed to cope with a band of lively youngsters. Others do not realize that they can be involved without having to do hands-on work, so do not put themselves forward. People are needed to take money, make drinks and collect materials for craft. Someone who wants to support the programme but does not feel able to work directly with the children can be an invaluable support by taking responsibility for one of these tasks.

Consider asking older people to help. Many retired people are grandparents and some do not see their families as often as they would like. They have a wealth of experience as well as time to offer. Young mothers who do not live near their own parents may welcome the chance to chat with an older and experienced person.

Teenage children often enjoy being helpers. Some schools allow their Year 12 and 13 students to help in a children's club as part of their community service.

There is detailed information on support and training for leaders and helpers in Chapter 9, 'Rules and resources'.

CHURCH SUPPORT

Having done your basic research and decided that your plan is viable, the next step is to take it to your clergy and church council. They are ultimately responsible for all work undertaken in the name of the church. You will need their permission to proceed, as well as prayerful support. It is sensible and courteous to discuss the project with your vicar or minister before going to the meeting. Write down as much information as possible and think through any likely questions. Make it clear from the outset what financial and other support you hope the church council will provide.

Some churches are happy to support a children's club financially as part of their evangelism programme. This will vary from being allowed to use the church hall without charge or for a nominal rent to being given an annual grant. Whatever the situation, you will need some funds for resources and refreshments, and maybe some equipment before you start.

Involving the congregation

Let the congregation know about your plans. Include them in the prayers each Sunday and in the church magazine. Use people's expertise and goodwill. This can range from legal advice in the case of a large project to designing flyers. Encourage everyone to own the project by providing money for T-shirts or an outing, or collecting scrap for craft activities. This way, everyone can be involved.

Most children's clubs are held midweek and during the day, so the congregation does not necessarily see them in action. It is vital that the church should own this work as part of its mission among children. Invite people who are available to pop in, or have a special session for visitors. Displays of photographs and a report in the church magazine are simple ways of making the event widely known. If you need cash, have a bucket collection after a service or invite people to sponsor equipment, books or toys.

CHRISTIAN CONTENT

The style of activities and level of Christian witness or teaching will depend on the children and the nature of the club. An after-school club on an urban housing estate will have a different ambience from one operating in the village school. A toddler club in an affluent suburb or multi-cultural area will be different from one that consists of post-baptismal families in a tight-knit community.

Any Christian teaching or worship must be appropriate for the age and understanding of the children. You cannot assume that the children or their parents will have any knowledge of the Christian faith, the Bible or prayer. Plan this part of the session very carefully. You will find detailed help in Chapter 3, 'Engagement and faith sharing', and the Centre Point, 'Worship: making God real'.

Make it clear on your publicity if your event will include simple Christian teaching or visits to the church. Respect children from other faiths and cultures and seek advice if necessary.

However you express it, whether by your witness or by more overt teaching, remember that you are handing down the story of God's loving relationship with his creation as told in scripture and the lives of Christians throughout the ages. This story continues today.

✛

TIME FOR REFLECTION

You probably have some indication about the direction in which your outreach among children is moving. Go through each section of this chapter again and note where you have come to some decisions and where you need to think further.

- With which people do you need to discuss your ideas?
- Where can you find the help that you need?
- Are you being realistic or are you in danger of taking on too much at once?

BIBLE LINK

LUKE 14:28–30

The Gospels are full of stories of people following Jesus. In most cases, it seems to be a sudden decision. They literally leap up and follow him along the road. Yet, time after time, Jesus warns about the price of discipleship, the need to weigh the costs and be prepared for the difficulties that lie ahead. One parable that is rarely quoted is the story of the man who plans to build a tower.

Suppose one of you wants to build a tower. What is the first thing you will do? Won't you sit down first and figure out how much it will cost and if you have enough money to pay for it? Otherwise, you will start building the tower, but not be able to finish. Then everyone who sees what is happening will laugh at you. They will say, 'You started building but could not finish the job!'

If you believe that God is calling your church to extend its ministry among children, you need to be wholehearted and plan your work carefully. We know that the choices we make, no matter how small the issue, can have large effects. They are the stuff of the kingdom of God.

Chapter 9

RULES AND RESOURCES

At first reading, the title of this chapter may seem to be a contradiction. Rules are made to hinder; resources are there to help. On the contrary, most legislation and guidelines exist to ensure the well-being of children and to see that adults who work with them are adequately supported. Paperwork is time-consuming but, once it is in place, most children's activities run smoothly and the leaders are properly equipped should problems arise.

If your church has well-established children's work already, most of this chapter will be familiar to you. New training opportunities and courses are appearing every few months, however, ranging from short workshops to extended validated courses, so it is worth reading the section on training thoroughly, even if you only skim through the rest.

The vast majority of legislation concerning children's welfare is common sense. Few parents, if any, would leave a youngster with a childminder without knowing that she was competent and that her home was safe. Most would meet the head teacher and check that the school had a satisfactory record before enrolling their child. We must demonstrate that children are valuable to the Church by offering equally high standards of nurture and care. Fortunately, there are numerous resources and organizations to help us.

HEALTH AND SAFETY

Every adult working with children should have been approved by the church council. Each denomination has its own guidelines, but approval will usually include an enhanced disclosure by the Criminal Records' Bureau. Information on this is provided in the section 'Legality and common sense' (p. 86).

Inform your church's insurers that the club is taking place. It is unlikely that there will be any extra charge but the insurers need to know if there are going to be outings or sporting activities.

Your local Early Years' Development office will be able to advise you on basic health and safety rulings and provide training on first aid and similar subjects. The staff are usually helpful and pleased to know of activities that support their work in the community.

If your club involves care of children of less than eight years old, for two hours or more a day, on six or more occasions during the year, you will need to register it with Ofsted. In practice, very few holiday clubs meet the requirements for this registration. It is advisable to contact the office anyway as legislation concerning care of children has changed several times in recent years.

Midweek and Saturday morning clubs usually have to be registered. This is advisable as the club can then benefit from grants, training and publicity.

NUMBERS OF ADULTS

Gear your programme to the numbers of leaders available, the premises and facilities. These will determine how many children you can accommodate. Different numbers of adults are needed according to the kind of club and activities taking place. The question to ask is whether your club exists to provide child care, or whether it is for educational purposes. Most clubs have an element of both.

The minimum recommended ratio of adults to children for a children's club is 1:8 for children aged eight years or older. You will need more adults if a variety of games and crafts are taking place simultaneously. Fewer adults are needed for an educational club where the children are working together in a formal situation, such as a choir or homework club, but there should always be at least two adults present in order to provide support and to deal with any emergencies.

Children under seven need an adult for every three or four children; one for every two toddlers is ideal.

If the children are going on an outing or having to walk some distance—for example, to play in a park—you will need more adults, with one for every pair of young children. Have firm rulings about lining up when crossing roads and see that adults hold the youngest children by the hand. Check that every parent has given written permission for the children to leave the premises.

Adults do not necessarily have to be directly involved with looking after the children. Seek out extra people who will help by taking the money, making drinks and clearing up.

AGE RANGE

Some clubs have clear rulings about the age of the children who may attend. Pre-schools operate for children aged two years and nine months to five years. Uniformed organizations have age-related sections. Most holiday and midweek programmes are geared towards children aged 7–11 years, but it is necessary to be flexible if families have one slightly younger child.

Decide what age range and number of children you will have in your club and plan the sessions accordingly. It is inadvisable to have children of less than five years in the same group as children over eleven years unless they have clearly designated areas and activities. In clubs with formal activities, the youngest children may need extra help with changing shoes, finding their places in books and so on.

LEGALITY AND COMMON SENSE

Your church should have signed up to the diocesan or denominational child protection policy. If it has not, this is the time to do so. The Home Office document, *Safe from Harm*, provides the following excellent criteria for selecting leaders and helpers.

- Previous experience of looking after or working with children.
- The ability to provide warm and consistent care.
- A willingness to respect the background and culture of all children in their care.
- A commitment to treat all children as individuals and with equal concern.
- Reasonable physical health, mental stability, integrity and flexibility.

All leaders should go through an enhanced Criminal Records Bureau check before having unsupervised contact with children. This procedure consists of providing basic information with supporting documentation, such as a driving licence, and is similar to filling in a passport application form. Most dioceses and denominations have procedures for making the application on the parish's behalf. It will take at least six weeks and up to three months for the application to be processed, so you need to organize this well in advance.

At present, helpers in short-term events such as fun mornings or holiday clubs do not need to have a CRB check. The church council should still approve the names of everyone who is helping, however, as it has overall responsibility for all work done in the name of the church. It is a good idea for any helpers who are going to be used regularly to undergo the check, so that they can take more responsibility in the future.

Local authorities and charities will give grants to groups only where the leaders have had a CRB check and undergone training. This is to ensure high standards of care.

SUPPORTING CHILDREN'S WORKERS

Every children's worker who has been through the CRB disclosure procedure and been accepted by the church council already has affirmation and support. That is only a start. Prayers and practical help are vital if that person is to undertake this work in the name of the church for any length of time.

Children's workers, like everyone else, need time off for illness, holidays or personal reasons, so keep a list of people who will help in an emergency. These may be former children's workers, parents or someone from another children's organization or another church. Knowing that help is at hand in an emergency does a great deal to prevent stress among workers and problems among the children.

Regular meetings to plan and evaluate work and time for training are also important. This is even more essential for a small group as more responsibility falls on each individual. Leaders and helpers should be prepared to discuss problems openly within the group and to praise or constructively criticize each other. The support of the vicar or minister is crucial in providing ongoing pastoral care but also to be on hand should there be a matter of concern.

TRAINING OF LEADERS AND HELPERS

It is now officially recognized that the care and education of children is too important to be left to chance. Childminders, carers and leaders of children's clubs do responsible and skilled jobs and it is now expected that they will be trained. A Christian club has a spiritual focus that requires special skills and values as well as the knowledge that every children's worker should have.

Nearly everyone who works with children in the church is voluntary. Some workers have a natural flair for looking after children or may have several of their own, and others work with children professionally. An increasing number of large churches are employing children's and young families' workers. Whatever the situation, our children deserve the best that we can offer, so every church should encourage its children's workers to attend appropriate training and should be prepared to provide financial support.

Training provided by Christian organizations

Diocesan or denominational children's advisers should offer advice on what training is available and provide their own courses. This will range from an extended course, such as *Fired Up... Not Burnt Out* (BRF) to short workshops or consultations. The availability and standard of training varies according to the area and annual programme.

Uniformed organizations have their own training schemes. Advice on running choirs and bell ringers is available from the Royal School of Church Music and the Central Council of Church Bell Ringers. Both organizations have regional associations.

Christian organizations such as Children Worldwide, Scripture Union and CPAS offer courses and workshops. Some of these extended courses are accredited at certificate or diploma level. A few Church of England dioceses have their own certificated courses, usually validated by the Open College Network.

Theological centres and Church colleges are beginning to develop courses in response to the increase in demand for accredited training in children's ministry. It is likely that more validated courses, including a degree in children's ministry and a system of monitoring standards, will be in place within the next five years.

Nationally recognized qualifications

Local colleges offer courses in subjects like Childcare and Education, Early Childhood Studies, and Play Work. They range from NVQ levels 2 and 3 to diplomas and advanced diplomas. There are both full-time and part-time courses, and modules can be selected to focus on the student's particular interests. Contact your local FE College for information.

Local authorities offer training for people who are working in registered children's clubs. It is always worth enquiring about training, even if your club is not registered, as the local authority may take any children's workers if the course is not fully subscribed. The most usual courses are an Advanced Certificate in Play Work, which provides the basis for an NVQ level 2 or 3, and courses like First Aid and Child Protection. Much of the work is practical and is assessed at the student's place of work. Courses are either free of charge or for a nominal fee. Your local Early Years' Officer will have details.

The Open University offers a short course, *Understanding Children*, as well as longer courses on various subjects concerned with education and child care. They operate at centres all over the UK.

Registered groups meeting frequently with children aged less than eight years usually require 50 per cent of the staff to have an NVQ level 3 or a similar qualification. The course is largely practical. It is held at a College of Further Education with visits to your place of work.

Hands-on training

Although there are academic courses, much training is hands-on and considerable credit is given for experience. The establishment of NVQs has opened the door to many people who have practical rather than written skills and had assumed that certificates and qualifications were 'not for them'.

It is worth being trained, even if it is not required, as it will give a greater understanding and interest in the work. A nationally recognized qualification would be useful should a volunteer worker decide to work professionally, maybe as a classroom assistant or a childminder, start to train as a teacher or move to another part of the country.

FINANCE

There are several sources of funding to support work with children in the community.

Government and local authority funding

- Local authorities will give grants to clubs if they fulfil certain criteria. Enquire about this when informing the Early Years' Development officer about the club.
- Large projects can receive funding for new work or for developing existing work with after-school projects. The Early Years' Development staff will advise on making a bid.
- In rural areas, the parish council, district council and the regional countryside agency often give grants for holiday clubs. They sometimes support ongoing projects.
- The police and local political parties sometimes give grants to help with clubs and play schemes. They recognize that the Church does a valuable job in providing a safe environment and lowering crime by running these events.

Charities

Charities provide a vast source of money and advice. Look at:

- Children's charities
- Educational charities
- Local church charities
- The Children's Fund
- The Church Urban Fund
- The Prince's Trust

Business sponsorship

- Most large businesses and local airports have a policy of providing funds for local projects.
- Small businesses and shops may help by providing goods at a reduced price or free of charge in exchange for publicity.
- Textile factories and paper mills are sources of large amounts of off-cuts and scraps.

Even if the sums saved are small, it is part of generating goodwill between the church and the community.

Membership fees

Always consider whether or not it is appropriate to charge a fee. A small charge for a membership card for a club that meets regularly guarantees a regular income and is a way of monitoring membership numbers.

Encourage prior booking for fun days and holiday clubs, maybe by charging extra for booking on the day. Make a small charge of anything from 50p to £2.00 per session according to your own costs. This helps with preparation and is a way of ensuring that the children value the club.

In cases of hardship, it is easy to offer membership at a reduced rate or a discount for large families. In some areas, it may be counter-productive to charge a fee. Decisions about this must be considered carefully in light of other local practices and the families' financial situations.

HUMAN RESOURCES

The best resources are people with a fire for children's ministry and experience of working among them. Teachers, social workers and nursery nurses have a wealth of knowledge that can be handed on. Carers, classroom assistants and parents often have far more wisdom and skills than they acknowledge.

PROGRAMMES AND HANDBOOKS

There are numerous programmes for holiday clubs or school-based activities but very few at present for extended midweek programmes or 'fun days'. They do tend, however, to be geared towards large groups and a particular style of teaching. If this suits you, well and good, but if you have a small group or few resources, consider material from CURBS (Children in URBan Situations), Rural Sunrise, and mission agencies such as CMS. Seek advice from your children's adviser or a more experienced church before choosing a programme. Personal recommendation is usually the best advice.

It is not necessary to use a published programme. If they do not fit with your aims and situation, create your own. This will take time but may be the best answer if you have someone with imaginative ideas and an experienced team.

Several Christian publishers produce paperback handbooks on aspects of children's work. Books on child development, education and play are available from the education sections of bookshops.

EQUIPMENT AND STATIONERY

High street shops are not the best places for buying resources or equipment, unless you only want small amounts. Local businesses will sometimes donate scrap paper and fabric or offer goods at a discount in exchange for publicity. Some Local Education Authorities will allow voluntary children's clubs to use their resources centres. This may involve paying an annual subscription but that is soon recouped by the saving made by buying goods at a greatly reduced rate. Staff should be available to advise you on what is suitable for your group.

Avoid buying large equipment unless you will use it frequently and have adequate storage space. Some councils will lend large toys and equipment or hire it out for a small fee. Some dioceses and youth organizations have resources centres with books, videos and small equipment like parachutes and badge machines for hire.

✝

TIME FOR REFLECTION

• Do we have high expectations of our children's work?
• Do we support our existing children's workers as well as we should?
• Do we encourage and support our workers to have training and make maximum use of resources?

BIBLE LINK

JOHN 10:10 AND 14–16

Jesus promised us life in all its fullness. We have already used this phrase as one expression of the underlying aim of our evangelism among children.

Jesus said: I came so that everyone would have life, and have it fully... I am the good shepherd. I know my sheep, and they know me. Just as the Father knows me, I know the Father, and I give up my life for my sheep. I have other sheep that are not in this sheep pen. I must bring them together too, when they hear my voice. Then there will be one flock of sheep and one shepherd.

Life means allowing our children to grow as whole people, physically, mentally and spiritually, without fear or neglect or unnecessary suffering. Helping in this growth is part of our living out of our baptismal calling to proclaim the gospel to every generation. It is a huge responsibility, but it is also a privilege.

CENTRE POINT

WORSHIP:
MAKING GOD REAL

WORSHIP: MAKING GOD REAL

Worship is as much part of planning evangelistic work among children as any research, strategy or use of resources. In Chapter 2, 'Back to where we started', we explored what we meant by the term 'evangelism'. One of the descriptions was about having a relationship with God so that 'when God puts his hand on a child's shoulder, and calls his or her name... that child will be able to recognize his voice and will know how to respond to it'. Worship is about that relationship.

Worship can be described as putting oneself consciously into the presence of God. It is something that is bound up with our whole lives. It can be done at any time and in any place or situation, tragic or joyful, but is most compelling when a group of Christians meet together to worship. Children need to encounter worship, to know that God is great and wonderful and that he loves each one of us unconditionally. They also need to experience worship as being part of belonging to a Christian community.

THE PRESENCE OF GOD

Telling God's story and our own personal stories is an essential part of any Christian nurture. It is equally important to give children a sense of the presence of God and assure them that he is with them at all times. A question to ask yourself at the end of every session, along with all the ones about success and enjoyment, is, 'Did each child have an opportunity to have an encounter with the living God?'

We have already discussed in Chapter 3, 'Engagement and faith sharing', that the level of Christian witness and teaching depends on the situation and the children involved. A vital part of it involves recognizing and valuing each child's individual experience of life and the spiritual journey that he or she has already undertaken. These experiences in the context of the child's family and school will influence the way that we offer worship with children who may have little or no experience of praying or the presence of God in their lives. Of one thing we can be certain: the God whom we can call 'Abba, Father', which can be translated as 'Daddy' or 'Dad', longs for his children to speak his name.

Introducing children to the Christian faith, whether by witness or direct teaching, is part of our ministry. Giving them an experience of the presence of God is the most precious thing that we can do, but it is often neglected. Prayers gabbled while the children sit silently in a huddle on the floor or round untidy tables do nothing to build a child's relationship with God or encourage personal prayer. Herding the children into church for a few prayers read out of a book is often the low point of the session and may do more harm than good. Helping a child to pray is a valuable gift that should accompany him or her for the rest of life's journey. A lack-lustre or badly prepared piece of worship feeds nobody.

Let's spend some time reviewing how we can help children to have a sense of the presence of God.

SACRED SPACE

If your activity takes place in a large hall, set aside an area for worship or sacred space. This can be as simple as a corner or alcove with cushions and a display. Make it as attractive as possible and invite the children to go there at any time. If you are using the church building, consider whether you will take this opportunity to turn a corner into a children's chapel, with low chairs or cushions, children's books and toys and an altar or table with a special display. If you are using the main part of the church, create an area where the children can sit on cushions or hassocks and you can be seated near them without letting the altar, table or lectern separate you from them. The sanctuary is often a good place because it is a defined space and usually carpeted. If you use it, sit in front of the altar or table with the children rather than standing behind it. This will give a sense of togetherness and let the children make eye contact without having to crane their heads upwards to see you.

Focus

Have a focal point for your worship. This may be a table with a cross and candles or a Bible. Lighting a candle before prayer helps us to remember that Jesus is the light of the world and provides a focus. Children love candlelight. A display relating to the theme of the activity helps us to offer it to God. Flowers, glass and pebbles help us to recall the beauty of his creation. Coloured material can reflect the liturgical season or theme of the programme. Most children's programmes are exciting and use bright colours. When it comes to a time for reflection, it may be appropriate to use the more pastel shades, reserving bright colours for special effects—gold for kingship, red for the Holy Spirit, green for new life and so on.

PREPARATION FOR WORSHIP

Worship tends to come at the end of a session. Prepare the children for it by setting a calmer atmosphere. This can be through packing up quietly together or having a news time or a story. Speak deliberately and calmly, and move slowly to lower any tension or excitement: most children will respond. Take time to lower the excitement and activity of the group before going into the sacred space or church, or just to sit quietly if space is very limited. Ask a helper to act as a doorkeeper to invite each child to go in when he or she is ready. Music played quietly will help to relax excited children, lower any tensions and set a tranquil atmosphere. Seating the children around a space such as the edge of a carpet or on a circle of cushions helps them to be calm. It may take time and patience but they will eventually know what is expected of them. They have to sit still and silently at school at times, so this is more familiar than you may expect.

As you read the last paragraph, you may have thought, 'That would not work with my group. There are too many children; they would never keep still!' Try it and see. Your own body language and speech are the biggest help. People speak at a higher pitch and more quickly when they are nervous or anxious. Smile and make eye contact with the children, especially any who are not well-behaved, so that each child knows that, whatever has gone before, this is a special time and you are glad that he or she is sharing it with you.

Never exclude a child from worship for bad behaviour or suggest that he or she is not valuable to God for any reason. The damage from such a comment could be irreparable. Gathering together for worship is a good time for a child to make a fresh start and be welcomed back into the group. Better to risk a few wriggles than for a child to believe that he or she is beyond the love of God.

PRAYING TOGETHER

Lighting a candle is an effective way of showing that the worship is about to begin. If you prefer it, using a simple stilling exercise such as the traditional 'hands together, eyes closed' for the prayer time may be helpful. Seek to give the children an awareness of the presence of God and his love for each one of them. If this is a new experience for the group, linking the activities to God's presence may be helpful.

If the group meets every week, take the opportunity to teach the children the Lord's Prayer and maybe make up your own group prayer.

Thank you; please

The simplest form of prayer is for the children to say the things that have happened recently for which they want to thank God, and then the things that they want to ask him. They may not want to speak aloud so give the children space to make their prayers in the silence of their hearts. This allows them to pray as they wish while being part of the community. Sum up the petitions by saying the Lord's Prayer together. If the children have not yet learned the prayer, they can join in by saying 'Amen'.

MULTI-TASKED WORSHIP

Most acts of worship are linear. We all move together from one item to the next, often after instructions like, 'Let us pray together' or, 'Now we will all stand to sing'. The only interchange is between the person leading the worship and the corporate response of the people assembled. We move from the opening greeting or hymn to the final Amen. The message in this is clear: we are a community drawn together to worship God. Singing and praying together is part of our relationship with God but also with each other.

But this is not how most young people operate today! As we have discussed in the first chapter and touched upon in the previous section, children are used to doing highly individualistic tasks, maybe several at a time. When they plan worship it tends to be like that as well, with several different kinds of worship going on at once, rather like workshops. This being so, perhaps having every child sitting or standing together and doing the same things together is not the only or even the best way for children to discover the presence of God.

Liquid worship

When you know the children, develop the idea of them offering their own petitions through prayer activities. They can be options within the whole programme so that the children can do a prayer activity or just pray on their own between choosing other things.

With older children who are used to this kind of prayer, have a series of prayer activities going on at once. This is often known as 'liquid worship'. It will enable each child to pray in the way that he or she finds most helpful and take as much or little time as he or she needs.

It could be an effective part of all-age worship or as the final session of a whole day event, starting with a brief introduction to set the scene and finishing with a final prayer or with each person leaving as they wish.

The following very simple suggestions for prayer activities can be used with children of most ages as well as adults.

Balloon prayers

Write or draw a prayer on a small piece of paper and attach it with a string to an inflated balloon. Most children will need an adult to help them do this, especially if the balloons have been blown up with a helium pump. Arrange for another adult to collect them in a bunch or a net. Finish your worship by taking them out into your churchyard or any open space and release them into the heavens. Knowing that the people who find them may be urged to share in the prayer or, at the very least, will be aware that there are children who are praying for the needs of the world, is a strong witness to our faith.

Beads on a string

Beads have been used as an aid to prayer for centuries and in several religions. Take a length of thick thread and some beads of different colours. Tie the beads on to the thread to represent your life—your family, friends, school, hobbies and so on. Use the different colours to mark the different people or events. You could also make a string of your life story, starting with your birth and going beyond the present to your hopes and fears for the future.

Tie the ends of the string together or leave it as a line. Use the beads to remind you to thank God for his blessings and to tell him about the difficult and sad things.

Boards and boxes

Have a board, some paper and felt-tipped pens in the church or the sacred space so that the children can write or draw prayers. Their prayer might be a drawing or a name: God will know what is in the person's heart. Some churches have a prayer board or box where people can post particular intercessions that can be used in a similar way. Show it to the children or make your own.

Catalyst prayers

Create several displays or activities that will act as catalysts to prayer, with one or two questions or statements beside them, for example:

- A clock, stopwatch or timer: How much of your time do you give to God? How do you use the time that God has given you?
- Stones and a cross or crucifix: Are there things in your life that trouble you or make you sad? Take a stone to represent them, hold it, and then place it at the foot of the cross.
- An electric fan and a balloon: The Holy Spirit is like the wind. We cannot see the wind but we can feel its power. Blow up the balloon. Feel the power coming from the fan.
- Cuttings from newspapers and magazines: Pray for one place or situation that is in the news at present.
- A bowl of water: We need water to live. It makes things grow, cleans and refreshes us. How do you use water? Jesus said he would give us the water of life. What does that mean to you?

Invite the children to pause by a display and do the activity or think about the question. A further option would be to write or draw a prayer on a Post-it to stick on to a prayer board. These can be offered at the final worship of the event.

God's story, my story

Each one of us is unique, made individually by God. Each one of us has a story. Cut sheets of A4 paper lengthwise into four strips. Invite the children to write or draw about themselves on a strip. Fasten the strips to make a paper chain. Use it to decorate the sacred space or place it in church.

Post-it prayers

Write or draw prayers on small pieces of card and place them on the altar table or in front of the cross. Write love prayers on hearts and put them in front of the Christmas crib, a picture of Jesus or a map of the world. Whatever the children offer, it is important to remember that these are their personal communications with God and not to be commented on or assessed.

The forgiveness tree

Recalling that Jesus died for our sins features strongly in some worship. This is especially so in Lent and Holy Week. This is central to our faith but, badly handled, can lead to inappropriate guilt and resentment. Children need to know that God can heal us from everything that spoils our relationship with him and each other and give us a fresh start.

Make a 'forgiveness tree' by writing the things that spoil our relationship with God and each other (personal sins or the sins of the world) on brown paper leaves. Lightly fasten them to a dead branch of a tree with touches of a glue stick. Say a short prayer of sorrow and then one for God's forgiveness. While this is said, shake the leaves off the branch to illustrate God's removal of the burden of sin. Then decorate the tree with paper flowers to symbolize God's gift of new life. An added piece of fun is to burn the 'sins' afterwards and celebrate God's forgiveness with a drink and biscuits.

Walking with God

Take a small group out for a walk, to the park or the shops or just down the road. Invite the children to look for signs of God while you are on the journey. They will see him in a variety of ways: flowers, clouds, people, behaviour, the wind, even cracks in paving stones can be signs of God and lead us to a sense of his presence. Remember to have parental permission to take children off the premises and enough adults to escort them safely. There is information on this in Chapter 9, 'Rules and resources'.

MUSIC

Music should play a large part in your worship. Taped music can do much to set the atmosphere before and during worship.

If you are following a particular programme, it will probably include special songs. These can be used as part of worship or to begin or end the session. If you need to choose some music, find out what hymns or songs are used at your local school. That will ensure that the music is suitable for young children and that a few of them will know it already.

Gathering songs

Consider having a 'gathering song' as the group assembles. When some of the children have arrived, turn down any recorded music and start to sing a simple repetitive song like 'Father we adore you' or 'Kum ba yah'. As the other children come into the space, they will join in. When the whole group is present, set the atmosphere by singing a last verse very quietly, even humming, and then having a few seconds of silence. If you have a very large group, you will not be able to sit them in a circle on the floor, so it may be better to seat them on chairs or in pews. Try to give them plenty of space in order to create a relaxed atmosphere.

Choice of songs and hymns

Many youngsters enjoy songs that can be sung from memory such as Taizé chants and songs with repetitive words or choruses. If you have two people with clear voices to lead the parts, rounds, canons and 'call and refrain' songs are always popular. Loud and rhythmic numbers are best reserved for large groups with an instrument to accompany them.

When choosing hymns or songs, look for:

- Tunes with distinctive melody lines
- Repetition of words
- Choruses
- Short lines and verses
- Christian words to well-known secular tunes—a practice that has been used for centuries

Using instruments

Instrumental music can set the mood for prayer or accompany singing. Singing unaccompanied is often the most effective way of learning songs and hymns, especially with small groups.

If the person leading the singing is also providing the accompaniment, a guitar or keyboard is easier than a piano because it is still possible to sit near the children and make eye contact.

Percussion or recorder playing could be one of the group activities and make a valuable contribution to the worship in this way. Making simple percussion instruments to play is a popular activity. Music is being squeezed out of the school curriculum so you would be giving the children an activity that they might not get anywhere else.

TIME FOR REFLECTION

- Have we seen worship as being at the heart of all of our work with children?
- How can we use our resources to give our children a sense of the presence of God?
- Can we provide worship that engages with today's children through imaginative use of prayer and music?

BIBLE LINK

This passage reminds us that the psalmist recognized the power of children's praises and that God longs to hear them worship him.

Our Lord and Ruler, your name is wonderful everywhere on earth! You let your glory be seen in the heavens above. With praises from children and tiny infants, you have built a fortress. It makes your enemies silent, and all who turn against you are left speechless.

Our Lord and Ruler, your name is wonderful everywhere on earth!

Think or discuss

- How can we let children be children when we worship together?
- How can we give them space and time to pray in the way that is natural for them?
- Do we believe that children may be closer to God than we are?
- Do we see our worship as something that belongs to adults where children are allowed in, or do we have a culture that welcomes all ages and stages of faith?
- What are the implications of this in our worship as a whole congregation and within our children's groups?

A FINAL THOUGHT

Bringing a child to know and enjoy the presence of God is one of the most valuable things we can do. Any personal relationship is precious. God loves each one of us unreservedly and everything may be offered to him in worship apart from anything that is sinful, for that in itself spoils our relationship with God. There is no right or wrong way. It is not for us to pass judgment on a child's offerings or to only offer the 'best' prayers or use the most able readers. We are privileged if we can help a child on a step towards God or to glimpse something of the relationship between him and his children.

PART THREE

OPPORTUNITIES
AND ACTIVITIES

Chapter 10

WORKING WITH SMALL GROUPS

As we have already read in the Introduction, it is suggested that about half of Anglican churches have no children and many more have very few youngsters. I hope that by the time you have reached this point in the book (unless you turned to this chapter before reading anything else), you will have reviewed the number of children with which your church has contact and be thinking about ways of developing the opportunities that have presented themselves. But although far more churches have ministries with children than is commonly recognized, some readers will be starting with no children at all, while others will have fewer than a dozen for a variety of reasons.

Here are some suggestions of ways to make the most of the small numbers that you do contact.

THINK POSITIVELY: SMALL IS BEAUTIFUL

Naturally, we want to have large and flourishing children's groups, but there are benefits as well as challenges in having a small number of children. You will have the opportunity to know and value every child as an individual. You can meet in a room, even in someone's house, which may be more comfortable than a hall. You will probably not have discipline problems and, if you decide to have an outing, you can travel on public transport or in a couple of cars.

When it comes to nurture and worship, every child will be able to take part according to their ages and abilities—one lighting a candle, another reading the Bible story, a third saying the group's special prayer, and another taking the collection. When there is discussion or open prayer, you will be able to encourage every child to contribute.

THINK REALISTICALLY: ADDRESS THE DIFFICULTIES

There are, however, many difficulties in having a small group. For a start, there are very few resources to support this sort of ministry. Most Sunday and holiday club programmes are designed for large and well-resourced groups and the activities are not always adaptable for a small group of children with few facilities. Even when they are, it can be disheartening to spend a large sum of money on a wonderful course, only to find that just a small part of it can be used as it stands. Leaders can feel very isolated, or even as if they have been set up to fail.

There are no perfect answers but here are several ways of addressing the issues:

- Always have at least two adults, however small the group.
- The children may be of a wide range of ages and abilities. Always prepare the work and worship just as carefully as if you had 50 children.
- Make sure that the oldest children are stretched and challenged. It is very easy to neglect their spiritual growth by using them as helpers or by giving them something less imaginative to do.
- Think carefully about what your aims are, and stick to them. Do not let yourself be pressurized into running a crèche at the same time as working with older children.
- For safety reasons, do not put children over eleven and youngsters of five and six together for active games.

THINK PRACTICALLY: USE THE SPACE

If you are meeting in the church hall, use the space imaginatively. Nothing is more depressing than a semi-circle of chairs in the far corner or around a radiator. Have an area for worship with a table set with flowers, a cross and Bible and maybe a candle. There are more suggestions on using this space in the Centre Point, 'Worship: making God real'. Put your craft table in another area, use a third, maybe with a rug or cushions, for storytelling and music, and keep a large space for games and so on.

THINK ABOUT SUNDAY

Although much of this book emphasizes the importance of being part of the church community throughout the week, it is equally important to provide worship and nurture that is appropriate for all ages on Sundays. Many children's leaders with only two or three children imagine that everything would be perfect if they had an influx of youngsters after a holiday club or if a new family joined the church. Others worry about how they would handle the new situation.

Make it clear what you are aiming to provide for your little bunch of children. Guard against being a glorified baby-minding service. While welcoming a parent who joins you with a restless youngster, never attempt to look after unaccompanied babies or toddlers while trying to nurture other children. Let every child take an active role in the worship. Lead the prayers by asking the children what they want to thank God for, and then what they want to tell him about, so that every child can offer petitions.

Prepare a version of the Gospel or other Bible story, using a large and attractive edition in a contemporary translation so that the children can see and share the pictures. Alternatively, use a large picture or other visual aid that everyone can see. If you are using a programme, choose one such as *Roots*, which is designed for a mixed age group. This is obtained on the Internet at www.rootsontheweb.com.

The oldest children

Encourage the oldest children to become part of the main congregation on some Sundays by giving out the books, reading, leading intercessions or serving. If they enjoy reading aloud or playing a musical instrument, let them contribute, but see that they have time to prepare the work. If they are not at ease listening to a children's Bible, offer a more advanced version that they can read at the same time. Remember to praise excellence when they have done something special, rather than dismissing it because the child is older than his companions are.

All ages together

Activities that can be shared by a mixed age group include making a collage, cooking bread or cakes, candle making, creating an Easter garden, finding things in the churchyard or church building, brass rubbing, songs and instrumental music. Craft activities like making puppets are also possible: for example, the youngest child can draw a face on a paper plate, which is fastened to a stick, while the eldest does something more elaborate.

What if the group is too small to be sustained?

If your group is just too small to sustain on a weekly basis, have a family service or an all-age Eucharist once a month and hold the children's group once a month. If children come on the alternate Sundays, encourage them to sit with their parents or with an adult who has been chosen by the church council to help guide them through the service. This will give the leaders time to worship without responsibility with the rest of the church family. Due to greater mobility and flexible working, the number of people who are in the same church on every Sunday is very small, but some families will make a special effort for a monthly service or event.

In order to support children in the church service, have the following at the back of the church:

- Someone who is ready to sit with a parent with several young children or unescorted youngsters.
- Children's service books and Communion cubes.

- Activity bags containing a picture book, a soft toy and so on for the youngest children.
- Activity pack containing a storybook with a worksheet for the older children.

Keep the bags and packs clean and regularly replenished.

See that the vicar or minister is aware of the mixed ages and is inclusive in his or her speaking and teaching. Also make sure that at least one hymn is straightforward, maybe with a chorus that the children can join in easily.

WHAT IF WE HAVE NO CHILDREN AT ALL?

Start by asking why! Is it because the children do not come to church or because there are literally very few children in your village or parish? The ways of addressing this difficulty differ according to your situation.

Very few children in the area

There is only one answer for this situation and that is co-operation. This is not always easy as joint activities are often seen as a con-fession of failure and a negation of present and past ministries. Sensitivity and affirmation is vital if any move towards collaboration beyond an occasional event is to be supported by the congregation as a whole.

Start by talking to your ecumenical colleagues or the other churches in your deanery. Consider providing a deanery or benefice group or working ecumenically. Examples of this are given in the case study 'KOS club' in Chapter 1, and in the section on fun days in Chapter 14, 'Holiday clubs and fun days'.

Some churches in rural areas run their children's work in a mobile caravan or bus that visits the different villages. Others have a car or minibus service that collects children and their families for a monthly service.

These kinds of initiatives involve imagination and co-operation.

Some may demand courage and sacrifice as a community lets go of non-viable children's work, but may well be best for the children.

Many of the following suggestions would also become viable with co-operation between churches.

Children everywhere, but not at church

Yet again, start with the children. Is it because there are only a few children living near your church, or is it because you are not providing activities that interest them, or that there are other things happening at the time you have chosen? If we assume that there are 40 children under twelve living in your parish, you should be able to have some kind of viable children's work, so undertake a review of the situation.

You may find that there are several very young children but few of school age. This often happens in places where there is new housing, suitable for first-time buyers. If that is the case, consider whether it would be better to start with a toddler club or a buggy service. Information on this is given in the following chapter on working with young children and their families.

Is Sunday the right day?

Question whether the best time and place is Sunday in the church building. If that were so, the children would probably be there already. Consider whether a club held after school or once a month on Saturday morning, or a short family service in the early evening, would be more appropriate.

If you are concentrating on school-aged children, start with a single event such as a Saturday fun morning or a short holiday club. Hold it where the children feel relaxed and at home, such as the local school or village hall. Distribute invitations to each child at the local school, and advertise it where children are to be found—the health centre or library or, in a small village, by posting leaflets with application forms through every door. In a compact community, you may be able to address the invitation personally to each child. The extra time will have been well spent because children love getting letters addressed to them.

Another development would be to have a midweek session or worship that is geared towards children instead. This may attract children who cannot or will not come to church on Sunday, so the dynamic will be very different. Link it with the entire church family by praying for the children's club on Sunday and praying for the main congregation at the club.

Include simple Christian worship and teaching as part of the event but remember that most of the children will probably not have any experience or knowledge of the Christian faith. On the other hand, they have all been blessed with a natural spirituality so build on their own experiences and progress slowly. There is guidance on this in Chapter 3, and in the Centre Point.

As the group or service develops, provide information about the life of the church, such as a copy of the magazine or notice sheet, for the children to take home. Have an occasional special service geared to this group—for example, Christingle, Mothering Sunday, Pentecost— maybe with refreshments afterwards.

Links with the rest of the church

Pray for any children's event on the preceding Sunday and include it on the Sunday after it has happened—maybe by displaying some of the work in the church or inviting the children to a special service with their families. Try not to be disappointed if some of the children do not come but ensure that the worship and nurture provided are of a standard to make any who do turn up want to come again.

If the event is held near to the church, one of the activities could be a 'treasure' hunt in the building. Many churches have stained-glass windows and memorial tablets. Nearly every Anglican church has an altar table or communion table, cross or crucifix, font, lectern, kneelers, robes and noticeboard.

✝

TIME FOR REFLECTION

- Do we really have no children? Do we only count the ones who come through the door on Sunday morning?
- Are we giving the best welcome and nurture to the few children we have?
- Do we value the few children that we have?
- Are we aware that reaching out to children and their families may involve change and taking risks?

BIBLE LINK

MATTHEW 18:19–20

Jesus said: I promise that when any two of you on earth agree about something you are praying for, my Father in heaven will do it for you. Whenever two or three of you come together in my name, I am there with you.

None of the suggestions and patterns outlined above is a perfect answer and, whatever is attempted, one vital component has to be present—the recognition that any group of children, meeting to worship God, is the Church. Praying at a toddler group or on a Saturday activity morning, or taking a carload of youngsters to the cathedral, are all ways of affirming the Christian community and need to be respected and recognized as such. If the activity includes worship, it should be recorded in the official register of services.

Leaders and, indeed, whole congregations may be disheartened at times when the future of the worshipping community looks bleak, but Jesus' promise remains true. The relationship between a leader and a small group of children, and the children with each other, is indeed a treasure and will bring its own rewards, not least a sense of Jesus' presence with them.

Chapter 11

CHILDREN UNDER FIVE
AND THEIR PARENTS

The majority of babies and very young children have some sort of contact with a church or a church building. Almost 25 per cent of babies are baptized in an Anglican church; many more are baptized or dedicated in churches of other denominations, or come to the services as guests. A number of health centres and pre-schools operate in church halls. Some churches provide services and activities for toddlers. For many churches, the main growth area is with children under five years and their families.

The increased demand for activities or clubs for children under five years stems from the government's moves to expand nursery and pre-school provision and establish Sure Start centres. Many mothers have fulfilling careers before starting their families and find parenthood very isolating. Given these opportunities, it is well worth exploring whether your church should make work with under-fives and their parents part of its outreach in the community.

BACKGROUND ISSUES

There are specific matters concerning parents of young children in which the Church can be involved, in the social as well as the religious context:

• There is widespread acceptance of the value in giving children an experience of worship from a young age.

- Some parents of newly baptized children genuinely want to keep their baptismal promises but need befriending and guidance.
- Much new housing is bought by young families who want to make friends and find out about the local community.
- Parents in poor accommodation need a place for their children to play.
- Childminders, nannies and au pairs value social contact with their colleagues.
- Community initiatives, such as Sure Start centres or privately run pre-schools, need premises from which to operate.
- Toddler groups are occasionally linked with adult education such as parenting, literacy and numeracy classes and domestic skills such as cooking.

STRUCTURED ACTIVITIES FOR UNDER-FIVES

Structured church-led groups for young children are pre-schools, toddler groups and pram or buggy services.

Pre-schools

Some churches have their own pre-schools or have a group operating on church premises. Now that the government has established nursery and pre-school places for most young children, the demand for new pre-schools is lessening over the country overall, but provision is still patchy. If you think that there is a shortage of places in your area and that you have facilities to offer, arrange a meeting with your local Early Years Officer before going further.

Pre-schools are inspected by Ofsted and standards are exacting but, if there is a need for a pre-school, you will be given all the help that you require. You could also get help from the Pre-School Learning Alliance (PLA). This is an umbrella organization linking pre-schools and supporting the active involvement of parents. It provides training and publications.

Since 1994, all pre-schools have to register as businesses or charities. As with any other church activity, the responsibility for a church pre-school lies with the church council. It will almost certainly delegate its responsibility to a sub-group and will appoint professional staff, but its name should appear on all legal and financial documents. A Christian pre-school should be an enormous asset to a church in that it has opportunities to offer simple worship and teaching as part of the curriculum, and can generate goodwill and provide pastoral support among the families that use it.

If there is already a pre-school using your hall or in the locality, arrange to visit the leader to discuss if there are any ways in which the church can be of service. Visitors and help from the church are usually welcomed but some leaders do not want to create links and this must be respected.

Toddler groups and pram or buggy services

Toddler groups and other activities for parents with babies and very young children are less formal than a pre-school in that they are usually independent and self-funding. However they are structured, they are:

- Links between church and the local community
- Informal events geared towards very young children
- Held at a convenient time for parents and carers
- A chance for children to experience worship and Bible stories from the earliest age
- A chance for parents and carers to meet, chat and discuss things that interest them
- Follow-up for post-baptism families

Although there are numerous books of activities for pre-school aged children, there is very little provided for toddler clubs and pram or buggy services. They all need planning, time and resources so information on setting up and running these groups is given in Chapter 12, 'Toddler groups and buggy services'.

POST-BAPTISMAL FOLLOW-UP

Toddler groups and buggy services provide excellent ways in which post-baptismal families can keep links with the church. Simpler forms of follow-up include the following:

- Sending a card on the anniversary of baptism and then an invitation to join the Sunday club or family service when the child is about four years old.
- Having a service and tea for all the families whose children have been baptized in the last few years. The exact timing would depend on numbers. Some churches may have only four baptisms each year; others have 40.
- Offering pastoral links with other young families—ranging from a friendship group to pairing a family with another one whose child has already been baptized.
- Sending personalized invitations to special services such as Mothering Sunday, Christingle or the Crib service.

SUNDAY AND SPECIAL SERVICES

Children have been regarded in different ways in each century and culture. The way that Jesus treated them was revolutionary to the society in which he lived. He cuddled the children at the street corner and called them signs of the kingdom. Yet it is assumed by some people that children cannot join fully in the church's worship until they behave and understand as adults. This is surely a contradiction of Jesus' teaching. Children's spiritual development starts long before they can talk or read books, so it is right that they should join in worship in their own way from the earliest age.

Let them be children

If we are going to welcome babies and toddlers with their parents to our services, we need to recognize that children do not behave in the same way as adults. They need to see and sometimes to move. Moving may occasionally mean a toddler taking a run up the aisle to be nearer to the action, but this is part of being a child. With guidance and a good example from the adult congregation, youngsters soon learn what behaviour is expected of them. Most presiding ministers, service leaders or preachers are not fazed by the odd shout or cry.

Crèche areas

It makes sense to have information on how to cater for young children if they become restless. A crèche area at the back of church, or near to the loos if you have any, is useful in allowing babies to crawl about safely when they have had enough of the buggy or the pew.

The simplest way to make a crèche is by removing one or two pews in a side aisle and then turning the next one around so that the seats face each other. Place one of the spare pews at right angles to make the third side with a gate. The area should be carpeted for safety. The space under the pews can be used as storage for soft toys, and there is ready-made seating for adults or older children. In this way, nobody is excluded from the worship.

ACTION

- Genuinely welcome young families and offer information on making babies and young children feel at home in church. The Mothers' Union provides a series of excellent leaflets.
- Consider having designated people to befriend parents with young children by sitting near or with them. Sides-people and stewards can help as well.
- If you are leading a service, make it clear that babies and toddlers do not disturb you. A light comment or even breaking off to smile or speak to a toddler will defuse any tension and reassure parents.

- Have soft toys and coloured picture books for children to look at. Provide children's communion books and cubes so that parents can help their children to follow the service.
- Ensure that the same support is available at baptisms and weddings.
- Have short services geared towards children on Mothering Sunday, Christmas Eve and other occasions, as well as family services.

✛

TIME FOR REFLECTION

- Think about the young children and their parents who visit your church building for any reason. Are there ways in which the Christian community can welcome or support them?
- Imagine that you are a young parent bringing a baby and a toddler to a church service for the first time. How would you feel? What help would be there?

BIBLE LINK

ISAIAH 55:6 and 8–11

God is hidden, yet close to us. Like the rain soaking the soil and producing fruits, his Spirit fills the hearts of his people and will produce divine fruits in his own time.

Turn to the Lord! He can still be found. Call out to God! He is near...

The Lord says: 'My thoughts and my ways are not like yours. Just as the heavens are higher than the earth, my thoughts and my ways are higher than yours. Rain and snow fall from the sky. But they don't return without watering the earth that produces seeds to plant and grain to eat. That's how it is with my words. They don't return to me without doing everything I sent them to do.'

Christian witness

We proclaim Christ by what we are rather than what we say. If our Christian community lives to proclaim the kingdom of God, then everything it does can have an evangelistic dimension. Welcoming and supporting a lone mother with several children, running a toddler group or helping in the local pre-school are a few of many ways of living out our baptismal calling to proclaim the gospel to every generation. Do not be disappointed if your efforts do not result in obvious conversions. The vast majority of adult 'converts' are actually returning to the faith that they were taught as children. Whatever you are providing will eventually lead to questions with ensuing interest and opportunities for proclamation and teaching.

Chapter 12

TODDLER GROUPS AND
BUGGY SERVICES

The previous chapter on children aged under five years and their parents reviewed the reasons why there is a demand for churches to engage with very young children and their parents or carers, and the ways in which they can be welcomed as part of the church family. This chapter provides practical help for organizing and running two of the most popular activities—toddler groups and buggy services. Although these two activities have a very different focus and structure, the overall requirements have much in common.

PREPARATION

Before starting up a toddler group or buggy service, research the situation and enlist the support of your church council. You will find information on this in Chapter 5, 'Partners in the community', and Chapter 6, 'Aims and audits'. It is not possible to run either activity on your own, so find at least one person who shares your vision and is willing to provide practical help before going forward. If your activity is to be an effective way of linking the church with part of the local community and providing a friendly place for parents and their young children to meet, it needs careful planning.

Start by asking the following questions and note down any that need further thought or research.

- Why is there a need for a toddler group or buggy service?
- What will be the aims of the group?
- How will the group be organized?
- Who will be the leaders and helpers?
- Where will the group be held?
- Will the intended venue have proper facilities, including storage?
- How will the group be funded?
- What resources (toys, drinks and so on) will be needed?
- What will be the best day and time?
- Having thought these things through, how do we envisage a typical session?

Choosing a name for the group

The original services for very young children were called 'Pram services'. As babies now tend to travel in slings, car seats and buggies, that is a rather outdated name, so this chapter refers to them as 'Buggy services'. 'Toddler group' is a more enduring title, but most churches give activities and worship for young children and their parents or carers another name—Little Bots (St Botolph's Church), Sunbeams, Noah's Ark, PTO (Parents, Toddlers and Others), to name a few.

Choosing the venue

This will be one of your first decisions, and the programme will be dependent on your facilities. You will need space for toys and other activities as well as a softly covered floor surrounded by chairs or pews to make a safe and contained area for the very youngest children. This will allow the children to crawl or toddle safely when they have had enough of sitting on their parents' knees.

Church hall or room

The obvious venue is the church hall or room if you have one. This will allow space for large toys, a soft area for the youngest children, and a defined area for circle and worship time. Remember that refreshments and a chat are an important part of any group for young parents, so see that there are kitchen and toilet facilities and adequate heating. It is also important to think about possible danger points. Check plug sockets, heaters, furniture, steps and so on.

In church

As most church buildings have stone floors with steps and pillars, it is easy to dismiss them as being unsuitable for this sort of activity, but think again. If you have chairs or movable pews, it may be possible to create an area with a rug and hassocks in the middle. The sanctuary and chancel are often suitable because they are defined areas and usually carpeted. Some churches have removed pews at the back of the church to provide a small meeting area or have created one under the tower or in the narthex.

Starting a buggy service may be a good reason for creating a crèche area. Information on making a simple one is given in Chapter 11, 'Children under five and their parents', in the section on Sunday and special services.

In the community

The big advantage of using the church or hall is that it brings parents and children into the church building and breaks down any barriers of strangeness. It becomes a familiar and friendly place. If, however, the buildings do not adapt easily or are cold, or situated on the edge of the neighbourhood, it would be better to hold the activity in the local school, village hall, library or health centre. These have the advantage of being familiar places where parents and carers congregate already. It is also true that many people will feel more relaxed in familiar surroundings.

In a house

If the group is very small, it could be held in a private house. This needs to be considered carefully, however, because not everyone wants to have a completely 'open door' to their homes. It would work best if the house had a separate conservatory or playroom. Safety issues and home insurance in case of accident or damage have to be well thought out if this is to be a regular event.

LEADERSHIP

Although one or two people can run a toddler group or buggy service, it is best if a small team of about four people are involved to share the tasks:

• Arranging chairs and putting out toys and activities
• Welcoming and chatting to parents
• Keeping a register and any other paperwork
• Telling a story
• Leading worship
• Providing refreshments
• Clearing up afterwards

Someone who is part of the baptism preparation group or the pre-school would be a familiar face to provide a link between families and the church by leading the worship, telling the story or welcoming parents. A person is more likely to accept an invitation to a group if it is accompanied with a reassuring 'I will be there.'

TODDLER GROUPS

Ownership

It is important that the group is run under the auspices of the church council. This will provide you with prayerful and financial support as well as legal protection. The council should take responsibility for insurance, appointment of leaders and helpers, ensuring that they have proper training and that the health and safety and child protection policies are in place. The church council should endorse the leaders' policies on the age range of children and ways of dealing with common problems and emotive subjects such as smoking and smacking. There also needs to be a clear policy about the Christian content and whether the sessions will include songs, Bible stories and celebration of Christian festivals as part of the programme. Resources to help with this are to be found at the end of this book (p. 169).

Paperwork

- Publicize your group in your health centre, doctor's surgery, school and supermarket as well as in the church and hall.
- Keep an eye on newly purchased houses near your home for signs of babies or children, and use them as an excuse to visit and offer an invitation.
- Prepare a welcome leaflet for new members and visitors to your church.
- Have a simple registration form so that you can contact parents if a session has to be cancelled and so that you have a record of any medical conditions as well as the children's birthdays.
- Keep an inventory of all toys and equipment for insurance purposes.
- Provide a short annual report and accounts to present at the church AGM.

Finance

Even the smallest group needs to pay for premises, resources, drinks and biscuits. Your church council should provide some support as part of its evangelism and children's work. It could allow you to use premises rent-free or for a low rent that covers costs. The congregation could help by providing toys or resources for craft activities.

Local authorities may want to include your club as part of their Sure Start programme. Contact the Early Years' Officer to enquire about financial help.

Other sources of funding and membership fees are discussed in Chapter 9, 'Rules and resources'.

Programme

Arrange for the group to meet at a time that links with dropping children off or collecting them from school. Allow time for parents to walk at a leisurely speed. Decide whether to hold the group every week in term-time, and which day would be most popular.

Even the most informal of groups needs a routine. The following framework may be useful:

- Children and parents arrive and are welcomed.
- Free play with toys, maybe with a craft activity for the older children.
- Children have refreshments at a special area, preferably with tables, supervised by parents.
- Parents have refreshments while children play or have singing time.
- Clear up and assemble in soft area or a circle.
- Circle time: story and/or worship.
- Notices and special news such as birthdays.
- Home time.

Christian input

Only you will know what is an appropriate level of Christian teaching. Songs can include Christian choruses as well as nursery rhymes. The story may sometimes be a Bible story. Some groups always have a prayer. Others may include invitations to special services or events. A few introduce parents and children to the church building by taking the group there to see the Christmas crib, Easter garden or other special features.

BUGGY SERVICES

A buggy or pram service has some things in common with a toddler group in that it is geared towards very young children, but the emphasis is on worship. Some buggy services only last about 20 minutes. Others will include playtime, toys and may even be held as part of a toddler group session.

It is best to start by holding buggy services three or four times a year to coincide with festivals like Christmas, Easter and Harvest, or to link with the beginning or end of term. See that the services are well publicized at the school, pre-school, health centre, supermarket and anywhere else where young parents meet.

The design of the service will depend on the age of the children present. If most of them are under 18 months, they will probably be happy to sit on their parent's lap or crawl or toddle in the area. If the majority are about three years, you may wish to extend the service by having simple craft activities or hold it during an ordinary toddler group meeting.

There are several books of prayers and stories for very young children but few service books. It is easy to create your own format, however. A typical service could be something like this:

- Have the worship area prepared with music playing to set the scene
- Parents and children welcomed at the door and invited to move into the worship area
- Greeting and introduction of the topic
- First song
- Story or activity
- Second song
- Prayer with the Lord's Prayer
- Announcements, including special events like birthdays
- Final song and blessing
- Music while people depart or have tea and a chat

The first and last songs could be greeting and goodbye songs that are sung each time. Very young children like to do actions and soon learn to join in choruses. Large picture books and pop-up books make good visual aids, but make sure you know the story well enough to tell it rather than read it. The parents may feel a little self-conscious at first with singing children's songs and doing actions, but encourage them to join in from the start so that it is their worship as much as the children's. A few parents will probably sit around the edge and chat. Encourage them to join in by helping their children with action songs, listening to the story and clearly saying, 'Amen' at the end of the prayer.

If you have a committed team and the energy, you could expand to a monthly service, maybe as part of one of the sessions of a toddler club. Make it clear that parents with babies are welcome to join in on these occasions. This will make a useful bridge for youngsters joining the club when they are old enough.

Make haste slowly

Some of the parents will genuinely want to bring their children up in a Christian atmosphere and want to keep their baptismal promises. Others have had negative experiences of religion or have stereotyped views about the way that Christians behave. They may feel that the Christian story is, if not untrue, irrelevant in today's world. Our job is not to force our own views down people's throats but to be Christ to those we meet.

A group that is led sensitively will allow time for questions and discussion. As we noted in the story of the Samaritan woman in Chapter 3, 'Engagement and faith sharing', we need to be prepared to be vulnerable and even challenged about our personal weaknesses and mistakes as well as those of the Church.

Some parents may start to enquire about the Christian faith because the atmosphere is informal and relaxed. Others may feel that, although they are not committed Christians themselves, they want their children to have an opportunity to hear the Christian story. This is something to celebrate.

Whatever steps you take, contact with young children and their families should never be used as a means of seeking converts but as an opportunity to demonstrate God's love for every child and adult through the witness of your local Christian community. There will be occasions when we can talk about our faith and enter into dialogue. Christian festivals, baptisms, and the offer of 'an upward thought' or prayer when a person is in need are wonderful opportunities and may be the preparation for the first steps of a journey of faith.

✛

TIME FOR REFLECTION

- Basic behaviour is laid down very early in a child's life. What does that say about the value of toddler groups and buggy services?
- If anyone asked you why you were considering starting a Christian toddler group, what would you reply?
- Have you ever felt pressurized by people who wanted to tell you about their faith? How did you feel? What was, in your view, inappropriate?
- When has discussing your joys and sorrows with a Christian been helpful? What made it so?

BIBLE LINK

LUKE 24:13–17a and 19–31

Our relationship with young parents involves walking alongside them and sharing in their joys and sorrows, as, indeed, Jesus did with two bereaved and confused friends on the road to Emmaus.

Two of Jesus' disciples were going to the village of Emmaus, which was about eleven kilometres from Jerusalem. As they were talking and thinking about what had happened, Jesus came near and started walking along beside them. But they did not know who he was.

Jesus asked them, 'What were you talking about as you walked along?'

… They answered: Those things that happened to Jesus from Nazareth. By what he did and said he showed that he was a powerful prophet, who pleased God and all the people. Then the chief priests and our leaders had him arrested and sentenced to die on a cross. We had hoped that he would be the one to set Israel free! But it has already been three days since all this happened. Some women in our group surprised us. They had gone to the tomb early in the morning, but did not find the body of Jesus. They came back, saying that they had seen a vision of angels who told them that he is alive. Some men from our group went to the tomb and found it just as the women had said. But they didn't see Jesus either.

Then Jesus asked the two disciples, 'Why can't you understand? How can you be so slow to believe all that the prophets said? Didn't you know that the Messiah would have to suffer before he was given his glory?' Jesus then explained everything written about himself in the Scriptures, beginning with the Law of Moses and the Books of the Prophets.

When the two of them came near the village where they were going, Jesus seemed to be going further. They begged him, 'Stay with us! It's already late and the sun is going down.' So Jesus went into the house to stay with them.

After Jesus sat down to eat, he took some bread. He blessed it and broke it. Then he gave it to them. At once they knew who he was, but he disappeared.

Seeing is believing

Luke's story has three themes—a journey, faith through seeing and hospitality.

We have discussed in this chapter as well as Chapter 3, 'Engagement and faith sharing', the importance of being alongside the children and parents we meet, of understanding their culture, the stresses of a fast-moving world on young people, as well as the joys and sorrows that everyone experiences at some time. We have emphasized the importance of helping children to 'see', that is, to meet God in us and in worship rather than just being taught about him. In the above passage, the disciples recite the story of Jesus but do not find faith. They listen to his teaching but do not understand him. It is only when they share a meal as friends that they eventually recognize him.

What are the implications of this for the young parents we meet?

Chapter 13

RELATIONSHIPS WITH LOCAL SCHOOLS

When someone is asked, 'Where do you find children?' the immediate answer most people give is, 'In school'. Every child attends school from the age of about five years. Almost every community has children of school age living in it and there is a primary school in the majority of parishes or benefices. It is sensible, therefore, to explore and give high priority to forging relationships with the local schools.

PART OF THE PARISH

Every school is set within a parish. That may seem obvious, but it serves to remind us that it is part of the parish's 'cure of souls' as much as any other group of people who live or work there. As we read in Chapter 2, 'Back to where we started', the Church played a major part in the founding of free education for all, and, even today, nearly a quarter of our children are educated in Church of England primary schools. An effective Church school is a Christian beacon in the community. The relationship between the parish church and its school can be a vital and rewarding one. There are also many opportunities for contact between churches of all denominations and all the schools in the locality.

A mutual relationship

A church usually approaches a local school by seeking ways that it can help the school and provide a Christian input and presence. As in any relationship, there is give and take on both sides. It is important to see your local school as a community that can be equally helpful to the church. As well as being full of children, schools offer an enormous amount of expertise in child development, psychology and a large number of specialist subjects, as well as general educational information. Their facilities, which may include a playing field, are designed for children and are usually maintained to a satisfactory standard. Schools have much to offer to a church and both communities can benefit from the relationship.

Sometimes a school may approach the local church for a variety of reasons. These will range from asking if it may use the building for a special service or as part of RE, history or English courses, to offering to support the church by holding a concert or other fundraising event. The school may feel that support from the church would be useful at a time of tragedy, or for pastoral support of staff and students. These opportunities should be positively welcomed.

Existing contacts

Most schools welcome visitors or help from local churches. There are probably links between the church and local school already, even if you are not aware of them. If it is a Church school, the incumbent will already be a member and maybe chairman of the governors. This will also include representatives of the parish and the Diocesan Board of Education. Children in the congregation may be pupils in any local school. Adults may work there, be governors, voluntary helpers or know children who attend the school.

RESOURCES

Having appraised the present relationships and contacts, your next step is to review your own resources. This needs a two-pronged approach. At the same time as looking at what you have to offer, you need to be aware of the school's own resources and the needs of the locality.

What do you have to offer to your local school? Is this something that it will find useful? The building is an obvious asset. It can be used for services, concerts and plays. It is a live RE lesson and may provide information on local history and architecture. Before offering this, however, think further. Ask whether the church is actually a better building than the school hall for worship and other events, and whether you have the resources to provide information and people to introduce an RE class to the church.

Taking assembly, teaching RE or providing pastoral support should have high priority. Be aware, however, that these tasks require preparation and visiting the school regularly, so are heavy commitments for clergy and lay leaders.

Do not restrict contact with the school to the clergy. Ask what other talents or time members of the congregation have that could possibly be of use to the school.

Find out what the school needs and see if you can match any of its requirements with the resources in your parish. This can range from offering help with particular lessons or activities to providing publicity for a school event. Ways of providing service and links with the school are listed later in this chapter.

THE HEAD TEACHER

Gaining the goodwill of the head teacher and governors is vital before you go any further with your plans or ideas. There is a far more positive attitude towards schools and churches working together than there was even five years ago, so you will probably be welcomed. Head teachers, however, are busy people. It is sensible and courteous to ask for an appointment and to make it clear what you would specifically like to discuss. Remember that you are a visitor and need the Head's permission to enter the school. If you do not know the school, ask about it and its children, its strengths and its needs. Be where the school is, not where you are.

Once you have met and agreed that there are ways that the church and school can work together, consider whether it would be helpful to invite the Head for a cup of tea or a meal as a more relaxed way of discussing the subject.

If you are having a meeting at church about your work with its children or young people, invite the head teacher to the meeting. The majority of Heads will attend or send a representative. They will have expert knowledge about children and young people and may know nearly every child in your parish. Most head teachers, whether practising Christians or not, are supportive of the social and moral dimension of the Church's work with children and young people.

Some head teachers do not wish to work with the church for a variety of reasons and this should be respected. We have to remember that some teachers have had negative experiences of Christian teaching or presence in school, either when they were children or as teachers. This is one of the reasons why we should always progress slowly and carefully with any work in the community. One bad assembly, some inappropriate teaching or too much pressure can cause damage that will not be forgotten.

Most head teachers would want to take any major decisions to the staff and governors before making a firm commitment anyway. Similarly, the church council should be kept fully informed about any developments.

OPPORTUNITIES FOR MISSION

A church needs to own its schools by making them part of its mission strategy in which every member can and should be involved. This should include the following aspects:

- Praying regularly on Sundays for the school's staff and children
- Including schools in any evangelism or development programme
- Using occasions like Education Sunday and the beginning of the school year to promote the importance of Christian education
- Ensuring that work in schools is an integral part of pastoral and teaching ministries
- Reporting on the work with schools at church council and annual meetings
- Encouraging members of the congregation to be active school governors
- Welcoming school groups to the church building for RE and related topics
- Inviting schools to display artwork or provide music for specific services
- Publicizing and supporting school events

WORSHIP AND SPIRITUALITY

Every school is required by law to have acts of worship, often called assemblies. They are subject to Ofsted inspection and have to follow a plan and have the outline and content recorded. Leading an act of worship can be far more difficult than teaching a lesson or preaching a sermon and needs careful preparation. Knowing the topics being studied, the time allowed and something about the children is vital. If you are regularly involved in leading acts of worship, it is advisable to attend the planning meeting each term.

Much worship that is offered in Church schools is an expression of the Christian ethos of the school and is both reflective and imaginative. Children have an opportunity to have an experience of God within a community where his name is honoured. A young mother from south London acknowledged at a church meeting, 'My daughter taught me to pray. She learned how to pray at school.'

Present-day RE lessons encourage use of religious artefacts and visits to places of worship to learn about the way that people practise their faith. It has been recognized that it is good for children to experience worship, so there is a new openness to clergy leading assemblies, or school services being held in church at Christmas and at the end of the school year. It is encouraging to find a general perception that far more parents are giving permission for their children to attend religious services than a decade ago. Examples of this are given at the end of this chapter.

THE CHRISTIAN COMMUNITY IN SCHOOL

The effects of goodwill between schools and churches have spread far beyond the children. Staff and parents have also been affected by the experience of worship through the school and, in some cases, it has been a first step in coming to faith.

Many parents will attend an act of worship in their children's school but would not feel at ease in a church building. Members of the congregation should attend major school services to emphasize their support of the school and to chat with the parents. Clergy need to be prepared for enquiries about the Christian faith to spring from such contact.

In 2000, a church on a housing estate ran an Emmaus course for a group of parents as a direct result of enquiries stemming from attending worship at the local Church school.

For many youngsters and, indeed, staff, the school's act of worship is 'Church' for them. The school needs to be recognized and respected as a worshipping community. This includes holding major services, including eucharistic worship and baptisms, in school as well as church, and ensuring that all school worship is of a high standard and priority.

Children's own experience of worship and the Christian environment of a Church school may lead them to evangelizing their own families and friends or wanting to make faith commitments themselves. We cannot overestimate the ministries of children among their families and friends.

A vicar in Essex found the parents of a child in his Controlled school on his doorstep one evening. 'We decided that we would allow our children to make up their own minds about religion. Our daughter has decided from what she has learned at school that she wants to be baptized. What do we do now?'

CHRISTIAN TEACHING

Christian teaching can be far more than the vicar or minister taking assembly or RE lessons, valuable though those ministries are. Members of the congregation with particular skills could help with Christian teaching. Consider the following options:

- Leading or helping with a school or class act of worship
- Helping to organize a special service at Christmas or for school leavers
- Teaching or assisting with RE lessons, including those held in church
- Providing ongoing pastoral support
- Leading a prayer group
- Running a Christian group during the lunch hour

As we have already discussed, these types of ministries involve a considerable commitment. Most of them will be built into the school's programme and the staff will expect the helpers to be reliable. On the other hand, most help of this type is appreciated and the helpers are regarded as real friends of the school.

OTHER HELP

The ways in which people can witness by involvement in a local school, without being directly involved in the worship or spiritual life, are numerous. Here are some examples:

- Being a school governor
- Helping with reading groups
- Paid or voluntary administrative work or midday supervision
- Helping in the classroom or with school outings
- Offering a particular skill like coaching a sport or playing a musical instrument
- Helping with school events

People who attend a church tend to want to support a Church school. Some of these tasks, however, might be of more service in a community school, where the helper could be the only Christian voice. They may not seem to be particularly Christian, but being 'Christ in the playground' is as valuable a part of witness as more overt teaching. Christian families with children in community or private schools provide a valuable ministry and Christian witness as governors or helpers.

WITNESS

As discussed at the beginning of Chapter 2, 'Back to where we started', evangelism is about witnessing by presence and the way that we live out our Christian lives as much as about overt teaching and faith sharing. Schools that welcome Christians as visitors or helpers do so in a spirit of trust. It is an abuse of that trust if contact with the children is used to attempt to proselytize or to invite children to a particular church. If you are in doubt about how to talk to children about your Christian faith during an RE lesson or in reply to questions, seek the help of a member of the teaching staff.

As we have already discussed at the end of Chapter 11, 'Children under five and their parents', our very presence in school and the help that we offer is a witness in itself and may well lead to questions and opportunities for discussion with the staff and parents that you meet. It is unfortunate that some small religious groups have targeted schools for their own ends, with a resulting breakdown of confidence between the teachers and any religious organization. We need to recognize the privilege of working with children and see that we take such responsibilities seriously.

SCHOOLS' WORKERS

Professional schools' workers are employed in some areas and their numbers are increasing. The story of one such project, 'Building bridges', is recorded in Chapter 5, 'Partners in the community'. Some schools' workers are funded by Christian charities such as Scripture Union; others are paid for by the churches in a deanery or as an ecumenical project in a locality. Their work is varied but is not unlike that of a school chaplain and may include the following:

- Leading acts of worship
- Taking or assisting in RE lessons
- Being involved in circle time or PSHE sessions
- Pastoral work with staff and students
- Being a listening ear for students with problems
- Running Christian groups or enquiry sessions like Youth Emmaus
- Using particular skills such as music, drama or sports' coaching

Some local charities will offer support with RE in schools. Your diocesan RE adviser will provide single sessions and INSET training. Organizations such as BRF will provide INSET training and creative arts days (*Barnabas Live*) linking RE with drama, dance, music and storytelling.

✦

TIME FOR REFLECTION

Think about your local school.

• What links do you have already?
• How can your church and school serve each other and the wider
  community?

BIBLE LINK

PSALM 78:1–7

My friends, I beg you to listen as I teach. I will give instruction and
explain the mystery of what happened long ago. These are the
things we learnt from our ancestors, and we will tell them to the
next generation. We won't keep secret the glorious deeds and the
mighty miracles of the Lord.

God gave his Law to Jacob's descendants, the people of Israel.
And he told our ancestors to teach their children, so that each
generation would know his Law and tell it to the next. Then they
would trust God and obey his teachings, without forgetting anything God had done.

ENCOURAGING DEVELOPMENTS

After over 30 years of neglect and even hostility towards the telling
of the Christian story in school, there is exciting and creative work
between churches and schools all over the country. In Durham, the
imaginative leavers' service for the Church primary schools proved
so popular that community schools asked if they could take part as
well. The result is that the education department holds five services

in the cathedral each July, with over a thousand children from Year 6 taking part.

In Worcester, after the success of their *JC 2000* millennium project, teachers asked for more help with teaching on symbols and worship, including Holy Communion. Ten large churches, including the cathedral, run *JC Today*, an exploration of the Eucharist and the symbols used in worship and the church building. Children take part in workshops on craft, dance, drama and music and these are fed into a final Eucharist. As well as the children, teachers and helpers benefiting, local clergy who attend them are being given the opportunity to break the mould in their own churches' worship through what they have experienced.

These are large projects led by talented teams from diocesan education departments, but they are examples of the overwhelming desire for schools to engage with churches in worship and RE in a way that has been unknown for several decades. Up and down the country, children are taking part in worship through links between the school and a local church. This gives us reason to rejoice and presents opportunities that every local church should grasp.

Chapter 14

HOLIDAY CLUBS AND FUN DAYS

The simplest way of starting activities for children outside the immediate church family is by having a single event such as a fun morning or a short holiday club. Although the basic plans are the same for either activity, the programmes will be very different.

Holiday clubs

Holiday clubs may last for any length of time between three mornings and five days. The programme tends to have a number of activities and games based on a theme or story. The objectives of a holiday club are usually a mixture of spiritual and social. There is a desire to reach children in the locality with the Christian story and to make Christ real to them. This is balanced with providing service in the community. According to the Family Holiday Association, a third of families in the UK cannot afford to go away for a holiday, so a club or play scheme is an excellent way of providing safe and imaginative play during the long summer holidays. Other children will also enjoy a structured time with their friends, whether their parents are at home or at work.

Fun days or mornings

A fun day is a single event that usually focuses on a particular subject or theme. There is an infinite variety of day or half-day events, all for different groups of people and with different intended outcomes. They range from festivals with several hundred children taking part to a small group of children meeting in the church hall for a couple of hours to work together on art and craft for the next Sunday's worship or just to enjoy a morning's games, songs and fellowship.

PREPARING FOR A HOLIDAY CLUB

After you have researched whether there is a need for a holiday club and made your initial plans, take them to the church council. You will need its permission to hold the event. You will also need its prayers and financial support. Involve the whole congregation by including the event in the prayers, asking for donations of resources for craft activities and for people to do jobs. Many people do not feel that they have the energy or skill to work directly with a lively bunch of youngsters but are delighted to contribute by taking the money, making drinks or designing the posters. Everyone can be involved by collecting items for use in craft activities such as jam jars, magazines, scraps of material, wool and coloured paper.

If this is your first event, use people and organizations to help you. You may find that there is someone in your congregation who has run a holiday club in another church, or a teacher who is used to planning this sort of event. If you do not feel that you have enough experience in your group, invite your diocesan or denominational children's adviser or an experienced leader from another church to help you with your planning.

Another option is to employ a Christian organization to run the club for you. This has the benefit of guaranteed high standards without an enormous amount of work on your part. On the other hand, it will not give so many opportunities for your church to forge relationships with the children who come to it. Discuss how you can work with the organization in the preparation and by providing helpers so that the church remains involved, and the experience will teach your own children's leaders how to run future clubs. Make sure that you agree with the aims and objectives of the programme.

Include an input into the Sunday service after the club ends and plan some kind of follow-up a few weeks later, so that you keep a link between the church and the children. This is especially important if the club is run by an outside organization or if the majority of the children have not had previous contact with the church.

Publicize the event. Put flyers in schools and places where children and young families meet. Include the name and contact number of the leader as well as providing a tear-off slip for booking. The booking slip should include space for parents' contact information and details of any medical conditions or special needs.

Finance

However simple the event, you will need money for craft materials and refreshments at the very least. Information on sources of funds and membership fees are discussed in Chapter 9, 'Rules and resources'.

Published programmes

The vast majority of holiday club programmes are geared to five sessions held during the summer holidays. There are a few shorter programmes designed for Holy Week or Easter. Some of them feature stories about Jesus or the apostles. Others are put in an adventure setting, with secret agents, pirates, jungles or a topical subject such as the Olympic games. They provide a lively programme with strong biblical teaching, including drama, music, action, craft and team-work. A list of examples is given in the Resources section on page 170.

Shorter programmes

Although most programmes can be adapted easily to four sessions, if your club is only going to operate for two or three sessions, including a day out or sports or a picnic for the families, you may find it has too much material. If you cannot find something of suitable length, and have an imaginative and experienced team, consider creating your own programme.

The simplest way is to have a two-part story or theme, one part for each day, linked by a common structure, songs, characters, a serialized story and so on, but with different craft activities and games. Sum up the programme by drawing the various elements together at the end of the second day or during the celebration or outing on the third and final day.

Holy Week

Many children's leaders claim that their most effective work is done during Holy Week. The events of Jesus' passion, death and resurrection form a strong and powerful story. The Western world has portrayed them through the arts for centuries, so it is carrying on the same tradition when our children explore them through art and craft, music, acting and storytelling. Foot washing, Passover meals, making bread or hot cross buns, a forgiveness tree (as described in the Centre Point, 'Worship: making God real') and Stations of the Cross are all popular ways of discovering more about Jesus' passion, death and then his resurrection.

Easter

It is a sad fact that the majority of the population does not know the reason why Christians celebrate Easter. As the festival always takes place during the school holidays (at the time of writing), even Church schools tend to neglect it. A great deal is taught about Lent and Holy Week but Easter is often forgotten once the last chocolate egg has been consumed on Easter day. Yet Eastertide lasts for seven weeks until Pentecost and there is a rich heritage of stories about Jesus' resurrection appearances and his commands to his followers.

Consider having a short holiday club in the week following Easter Sunday. The stories of Peter, the draft of fishes, 'doubting Thomas' and themes of new life, trust and discipleship provide plenty of material and allow children to explore the most important festival of the Christian year.

There are examples of recently published programmes for all seasons and occasions in the Resources section on page 170.

Worship in club programmes

Every holiday or midweek club programme contains worship. Elements of worship may be part of the club's mix of drama, games, crafts and Bible activities, or there may be a separate section of prayers and songs for the leaders to use as they wish. Some worship will include videos with testimonies. Whatever the style, it will have been carefully planned and is usually designed for a large number of children. It may be exactly what you require or you may feel that it is not appropriate for your particular group. For many children who come to our holiday and midweek clubs, this is their very first experience of worship or of the Christian story. It is common for a youngster to interrupt a leader to ask, 'Who is Jesus?'

It is advisable to start very gently with something like a few quiet moments at the end of the session to reflect on what the children have discovered and to assure them that they are in the presence of the God who loves them. You may find it helpful to use some of the ideas about creating a sacred space and offering a song and some simple prayers from the Centre Point, 'Worship: making God real'. Whatever you attempt, prepare it carefully and keep it short so that it is a pleasurable experience for the children.

Follow-up

Give each family a written invitation to a final event. This could be a picnic or party, or a service that incorporates the various activities. The service could be the final session or a family service on the Sunday with the crafts, songs and drama being included. If it is part of the Sunday worship, see that the artwork is well displayed and that your sidespeople are geared to welcome new families. Do not be disappointed if not everyone turns up. As we have already discussed, Sunday is a busy day with a large number of conflicting engagements.

Make sure that you have every child's contact details. After a few weeks, maybe at the autumn half-term after a summer club, invite them to a follow-up session so that the children and their families meet the leaders again. Display the photographs, sing the songs again and show a video of the highlights. Always include suitable refreshments.

Give out information about church activities and inform the families when the next similar event will be held. Consider keeping the addresses of everyone who has attended the club so that they can receive a special invitation to the next event.

RUNNING A FUN DAY

The organization of a fun day is similar to that of a holiday club, but the structure will be simpler. It may only last about two hours, so there will be no need to use a published programme. It will probably focus on a single topic—maybe the approaching season or festival—and it is comparatively simple to find activities that link to the subject.

The same health and safety guidelines have to be followed but there is probably no need to apply for grants or inspection, as the event is a single one. It is always sensible to ask people to book in advance but, with a single event, you can probably take bookings at the door, provided you have previously agreed how many children you will admit. If you are amazingly successful, with a queue stretching down the road, guard against the temptation to take too many children. This is a hard decision to make, but it is better to disappoint a few youngsters than to have overcrowding or, worse still, an accident. Word will soon get around that the fun days have high standards and are popular so that it is advisable to book in advance or turn up early. If they become so successful that you are always over-subscribed, consider having two identical sessions in the morning and the afternoon.

The reasons for holding fun days are varied. So are the clientele and the intended outcomes.

First step

If this is the church's first venture into outreach among the children in the community, a single morning is a good way to start. It allows the children to take part without being committed to several days. Inexperienced leaders may feel nervous about working with children, but will know that it will all be over after a couple of hours. If it goes well, and most short events do, the church can hold another one when it is ready. If there are things that could have gone better, there is time to improve them before attempting another event.

Activity days with a small group

A number of churches with a very few children or with poor facilities have abandoned the traditional Sunday group in favour of a series of activity days, usually held on Saturday mornings. They will include worship, teaching and activities around the subject, with time for refreshments and games. The session can be free-standing or can be linked with the next Sunday's theme so that the artwork can decorate the church and the songs or hymns can be repeated. This builds a bridge between the children's church and the main Sunday worship as well as preparing the children who may attend it. You will find an example, 'KOS club', at the end of Chapter 1, 'Being a child today'.

All ages together

This is similar to the above event but is more church-based. Adults and children work together on a particular project that prepares them for the following Sunday or the approaching season. This could include making a frontal for the altar for Harvest thanksgiving, baking bread for Holy Communion, learning seasonal music, making an Advent wreath, or having a penitential workshop that includes making palm crosses before Holy Week. The list is endless.

All churches together

Some churches have very few children. If, however, the churches of a district or a deanery combine forces to hold a fun day or festival, this will allow children to enjoy activities that they could not do in their own churches. Some cathedrals have family fun days or festivals organized by the education department, the diocesan children's adviser or the Mothers' Union. A single family can join in or the children can go as a group. It encourages them to build on the fact that there are more Christian children than they had realized. This also boosts the morale of the children's leaders, who can often feel discouraged.

Festivals need careful long-term preparation and a large number of volunteers. Allow at least six months and ask your children's adviser or people who have organized this sort of event to help you. It will be hard work but the rewards will be great.

TIME FOR REFLECTION

Holiday clubs and fun days are the most popular ways for churches to reach children in the community.

- Do we know about local or diocesan fun days and festivals?
- What sort of fun day could we run?
- If we already have a holiday club, could we improve it?

BIBLE LINK

PSALM 127:3

In the Bible, a lack of children is used to express sorrow, devastation and loss. A child was a sign of hope for the future.

Children are a blessing and a gift from the Lord.

Think or discuss

- Do we see our children as a blessing?
- Do we allow them to be children?
- Do we recognize the importance of play and God's presence in it?
- Do we believe that children have things to give as well as to receive?

JUNGLE JAMBOREE

The summer holiday club was about to start and the church had been transformed into a jungle. The centrepiece was a gazebo decorated with trees and plants to make a forest, animals twined around the pillars, and a waterfall of light blue fabric cascaded from the organ loft. Two children ran in excitedly, then paused, remembering that they were in church. 'That's all right,' said an elderly lady. 'This is God's playground. He wants you to enjoy playing in it.'

Chapter 15

MIDWEEK ACTIVITIES

Midweek clubs for children are a growing industry. According to the Kids' Club Network in 1994 (now 4Children), 4 per cent of children attended an after-school club. In 2002, it was 14 per cent, and the demand for places far exceeds supply.

Starting a midweek club of any kind is a major undertaking. Unlike a holiday club, which lasts a week and then the leaders can say thankfully that it is over until next year, the club will operate at least once a week during school term-time. Some may operate more often and for up to 51 weeks each year. This is an enormous commitment.

Midweek clubs fall into two main categories:

- Clubs that serve the community by providing child care combined with activities. Most of these operate after school but breakfast clubs are increasing.
- Clubs that cater for children with a particular interest. The most common are uniformed organizations, church choirs and bell ringers. Others include any subject where a group of youngsters and a couple of enthusiastic adults have a common interest, such as drama or five-a-side football.

Whatever the underlying aim, they are ways in which the Church can serve the community and give Christian witness with Christian teaching when appropriate. Providing a cooked breakfast for children may not seem to be an obvious way of bringing children and their families to faith, but witness often leads to questions with opportunities for proclamation and evangelism.

STARTING A MIDWEEK CLUB

Whatever kind of club you hold, there are three essential things that you need to do:

- Start slowly and gently, with small numbers. Extend the work when you are ready. A common danger is to overstretch your resources at the beginning in a rush of enthusiasm.
- See that you have a list of extra helpers to back you up in case of illness or other emergencies. They could include children's workers from other churches and organizations.
- Have a well-organized structure with long-term planning to support it.

As with considering a holiday club or a single event, research the need and plan your strategy for implementation. You will find advice on how to do this by working through Part Two of this book.

If, after careful consideration, you think that there is a need for after-school care or a breakfast club, sound out your vicar or minister and talk to your local authority's Early Years' Officer. You may think that the need is obvious, but work to address community needs may be already in hand, so you could be duplicating a service with a loss to both groups. There are also possibilities for partnership: maybe the local authority is looking for premises and could use yours, or it may know of another church that needs help to start a similar project. You may get a grant and will be offered training either free of charge or for a nominal sum.

SPECIAL INTEREST CLUBS

Uniformed organizations, church choirs and bell ringers are so much part of the backdrop of church life that it is easy to forget the valuable evangelistic work they do with children and young people.

Uniformed organizations

Brownies and Cubs, with their younger companions Beavers and Rainbows, and the junior section of the Boys' and Girls' Brigade, as well as smaller uniformed organizations, usually have some link with a church. Sponsored groups have a strong partnership with a Christian ethos and the vicar or minister involved in the choice of leaders and acting as chaplain.

Links with the church need to be valued and encouraged. The most obvious one is through attendance at a monthly all-age service or on St George's Day and Remembrance Sunday. A church leader can forge a relationship by helping the youngsters to take part in the service as readers or by leading the prayers. They can run stalls and activities at church events. In the wider community, youngsters in uniform with the church's name on it are providing valuable witness through service when they are washing cars or helping to pack bags in the supermarket.

It is always a good idea to build on what is known to be successful. Providing help to a uniformed organization may be a better use of limited resources than starting a new group.

Singers and ringers

Many youngsters have found that their entrance to the life of the church was through the choir vestry. Good worship has a strong evangelistic dimension and the faith is caught as well as taught. The pressure on a church choir is huge, with the demands of producing music every Sunday and attending at least one rehearsal each week, yet some churches still have flourishing children's choirs. In many others, however, it would be unrealistic to attempt that level of commitment. In that case, consider having a 'special choir' that meets each week, maybe after school, but only sings on special occasions—the family service, Christmas carols, Easter and so on.

Children on the fringe of the church may also be attracted by bell ringing or serving. As with singing, being part of the worship is a learning experience in itself and builds up the children's sense of self-worth and belonging to the Christian community.

PLANNING

Basic planning is the same for any children's activity. The following checklist is almost identical with that for a toddler group.

1. Why is there a need for a club?
2. What will be the aims of the club?
3. How will the club be organized?
4. What will be the age range of the children?
5. Who will be the leaders and helpers?
6. Where will the club meet? Will it have proper facilities?
7. How will the club be funded?
8. What resources will be needed?
9. What will be the best day and time?
10. How will the club link with the children going to or from school?

Having sketched out your plan, take it to your church council and follow the same procedures as for setting up a holiday club once you have its agreement.

STAFFING A MIDWEEK CLUB

There are four ways of organizing and staffing a midweek club.

1. Use your own volunteers. This has the advantages of being cheap and using people who are used to working together and are part of the church. Remember, however, that volunteers who happily forgo a week plus some planning time each year for a summer holiday club may find that sustaining a long-term programme and the commitment needed for a weekly event is too much.

2. People on the fringe of the church are sometimes willing to offer their services to the church if the subject is one that interests them. Leaders of uniformed organizations, organists and other musicians, and parents who have a particular interest such as football coaching are the most usual ones. Offers of help from the wider community should never be seen as second-best or brushed aside but should be grasped as opportunities for new relationships. Such goodwill is valuable and the appreciation from the church council may be evangelistic in itself.

3. Employ a professional leader and use voluntary helpers. Some churches are employing paid children's workers who would lead such activities as part of their work. Another option is that the leader is employed at an hourly rate. He or she plans the programme, takes charge of the resources and finance, and leads a team of helpers. It has to be made clear, however, that the leader is paid for taking responsibility for the club, not just for being there. A trained leader should guarantee high standards and provide an opportunity for the helpers to learn from his or her example and through training sessions.

4. Clubs that are held every day usually have paid staff. It is vital that a Christian organization should be a fair and honest employer. If the church council is not used to employing staff, take professional advice at every stage—drawing up a job description, the interview process and providing a contract. Denominational and diocesan offices will provide some information and will usually be involved in interviews. The trade union Amicus has a section for church workers and provides excellent advice.

If you use volunteers, be prepared to cover some costs. Have a fund for training and books connected with the work. If the helpers are retired or on limited incomes, they might appreciate being offered travel expenses.

Alternative management

A similar method is for the church council to delegate the work to an organization like the YMCA or a similar Christian group. This would be most appropriate with a group that operated frequently, and would be part of the organization's outreach in the area.

In some areas, there is a shortage of premises for breakfast and after-school clubs. If your hall is free and of a reasonable standard, you may be able to rent it to the local authority or another group and thus have a club on your premises without any of the work involved. It will be possible to form creative links similar to those between the church and its local pre-school or school. It should be seen as an opportunity for partnership with the community rather than a lesser option.

PROGRAMMES

There are now a few published programmes for after-school clubs. Examples are listed under 'Midweek ministry' in the Resources section on page 170. The programmes from CURBS (Children in URBan Situations) and Rural Sunrise are written with particular situations and cultures in mind. Others are similar in style and ethos to the American Kids Klubs founded by Bill Wilson.

It is possible to run your own programme by having a series of craft activities and games that the children can join in at will, a quiet area for homework with someone to help, and a story corner, as young children can get very tired at the end of the day.

Offer the children a snack when they arrive from school. Most children will not have eaten for nearly four hours and will need sustenance if they are not going to have a main meal until the evening. Provide water as well as sweet drinks, and fruit or crisps as well as biscuits.

CHRISTIAN TEACHING

Only you will know what level of direct Christian input is appropriate. This may be a short act of worship or a closing prayer. Information about church events could also be distributed.

Being aware of the needs of the world, having a termly charity and organizing fund-raising activities are all part of living the gospel and should be considered as important as direct teaching. Older children enjoy fund-raising activities like sponsored walks or sleepovers. Any child can contribute to simple activities like creating a mile of pennies or making cakes or cards to sell to raise funds.

Charities

Charities are always willing to give presentations or talks about their work. Many of them—for example, the Royal National Lifeboat Institution or the Children's Society—have speakers who are trained to work with children. Christian Aid, CMS and Mission to Seafarers provide excellent educational packs and teaching materials. The Children's Society provides an annual pack for a Christingle service.

SPECIAL EVENTS

Have an outside speaker or someone to teach a new skill to the group each term. Activities like pottery or cooking are popular. There may be someone living in the locality who can offer a couple of sessions to demonstrate or teach a particular craft. The police and fire brigade are sometimes willing to talk about their work or organize visits to the police or fire stations.

Outings, Christmas parties, Easter egg hunts, and other special events all add to the sense of celebration and community within the group. Be sensitive to family circumstances and provide help with costs if necessary.

OTHER HELP AND ADVICE

The charity 4Children (formerly known as Kids' Club Network) provides advice, training and publications, including *Getting it Right*, a pack of advice and guidelines for good practice for care schemes. It is worth becoming a member in order to be kept up to date with legislation and employment matters as well as using the training and materials. It has a very helpful phone advice service.

Rural Sunrise specializes in work with small and rural churches. The children's co-ordinator advises on strategic planning, fun days, holiday and after-school clubs. It has a set of biblically based resources.

Scripture Union runs Christian clubs in schools and the wider community. It has local field workers and will provide training, advice, and resources.

TRAINING OF LEADERS

Full information on training courses is given in Chapter 9, 'Rules and resources'. Paid leaders and, ideally, voluntary ones should have had basic training. Most local authorities offer an Advanced Certificate in Play Work. There are moves to encourage Christians to consider working with children as a career, by establishing accredited courses up to degree level in children's ministry. The majority of training, however, is far simpler and is accessible for a nominal fee or even free of charge. Diocesan staff and other organizations will run training days or provide consultations on a particular subject by request.

FINANCE

There is detailed information on finance in Chapter 9, 'Rules and resources'. It is worth remembering that local partnerships will give grants for new work or for developing existing work with after-school projects. Local projects are also supported by the Children's Fund. Enquire about making a bid when you discuss your plans with your local Early Years' Officer.

The club is part of the church's outreach in the community, so the church council should include some financial support in its budget. As with the other church-based activities we have discussed in this book, it could allow you to use premises rent-free or for a low rent that covers costs.

RAISING THE PROFILE

Most children's clubs are held during the day, so the congregation does not see them in action. It is vital that the church should own this work as part of its mission among children.

- Make the club accountable by asking the church council for a budget, however small.
- Keep the congregation informed by presenting a report at the AGM and writing regularly in the church magazine.
- Ask the clergy to include the club regularly in the prayers and the notices.
- Invite individuals to undertake to pray regularly for the club. This is a good way of keeping housebound people involved in the life of the church.
- Ask the clergy to spend a session with you and to commission new children's leaders at a meeting or during a Sunday service.
- Ask people with particular skills or hobbies to help with a specific activity.
- Make attractive displays of children's activities or work and put them in the church.
- Invite the children to services like Christingle and Mothering Sunday. Involve some children in them if possible.

✝

TIME FOR REFLECTION

The streets are full of children who have no knowledge of God as revealed in Jesus. Which is the way forward as we seek to engage with them and serve the wider community?

BIBLE LINK

MARK 9:36–37

Then Jesus made a child stand near him. He put his arm around the child and said, 'When you welcome even a child because of me, you welcome me. And when you welcome me, you welcome the one who sent me.'

Welcome a child

Children are too easily exploited and overlooked by adult society, and this includes the Church. But for Jesus, the child was a sign of the kingdom of God. Anyone who wants to share the values taught by Jesus must welcome and respect the smallest as much as, or even more than, the great and the strong. Behind the small and vulnerable child is Jesus, and behind him is 'the one who sent me'.

MISSION IS EXCITING!

A few months ago, I met a young priest whom I had known as a curate. He talked about his first parish—how the numbers were beginning to grow, the finances were not quite as bad as they had been and that he was now welcomed into the local school. Suddenly he burst out, 'Mission is so exciting!' Yes, it is, on the good days. There are times, however, when it feels like throwing pebbles into a deep black hole.

There has been a great deal of gloom and doom about falling numbers of children in the last decade, even a suggestion that the Church in this country will not be viable in a couple of generations. This is, I believe, a lack of recognition of the different ways in which groups of children and young families are being Church, and a negation of the power of the Holy Spirit to work within the people of God.

There is a new openness to religious experience; an acknowledgment that children's natural spirituality needs nurturing. Children's leaders are prepared to travel miles to get good training and demand usually exceeds supply. Church schools are places where the name of God is honoured, and the number of parishes that see their children's ministry as beyond the church walls and beyond Sunday is growing daily. These are signs of hope, but changing the way that the Church thinks about children is a long-term ministry.

If you are planning to start to reach out to the children in our streets, or to develop existing work, start where you are and not where you think you ought to be. Take small steps carefully and prayerfully and, in God's own time, there will be a harvest.

In 1991, only 15 per cent of children had any contact with a Christian church and the number was falling.[1]

In 2001, seven of the 43 dioceses in the Church of England recorded an increase in numbers of children and young people attending worship. The increase was significant in five of these dioceses.[2]

In 2002, 26 dioceses recorded an increase.[3]

It has been suggested that the tide is running out. On the contrary, the tide is turning.

NOTES

1 *All God's Children?* (1991)
2 *Church of England. Statistics for Mission. Attendance and Membership Figures* (2001)
3 *Church of England. Statistics for Mission. Attendance and Membership Figures* (2002)

RESOURCES

ORGANIZATIONS

4Children
Bellerive House
3 Muirfield Crescent
London
E14 9SZ
Tel: 020 7512 2112
www.4Children.org.uk

BRF
First Floor, Elsfield Hall
15–17 Elsfield Way
Oxford
OX2 8FG
Tel: 01865 319700
www.brf.org.uk

**Central Council of Church
Bell Ringers**
The Cottage
School Hill
Warnham
Horsham
West Sussex
RH12 3QN
Tel: 01403 269 743
www.cccbr.org.uk

The Children's Society
Edward Rudolf House
Margery Street
London
WC1X 0JL
Tel: 020 7841 4400
www.the-childrens-society.org.uk

Children Worldwide
Dalesdown
Honeybridge Lane
Dial Post
Horsham
West Sussex
RH13 8NZ
Tel: 01403 7101712
www.childrenworldwide.co.uk

Church Mission Society (CMS)
Partnership House
157 Waterloo Road
London
SE1 8XA
Tel: 020 7928 8681
www.cms-uk.org

CPAS
Athena Drive
Tachbrook Park
Warwick
CV34 6NG
Tel: 01926 334242
www.cpas.org.uk

Crusaders
Kestin House
Crescent Road
Luton
Bedfordshire
LU2 OAH
Tel: 01582 589850
www.crusaders.org.uk

CURBS
4 Hawksmoor Close
London
E6 5SL
Tel: 07941 336 589
www.curbsproject.org.uk

Mission to Seafarers
St Michael Paternoster Royal
College Hill
London
EC4R 2RL
Tel: 020 7248 5202
www.missiontoseafarers.org

Pre-School Learning Alliance (PLA)
69 Kings Cross Road
London
WC1X 9LL
Tel: 020 7833 0991
www.pre-school.org.uk

Royal School of Church Music
Cleveland Lodge
Westhumble
Dorking
Surrey
RH5 6BW
Tel: 01306 872800
www.rscm.com

Rural Sunrise
2 The Old Forge
Hailsham
East Sussex
BN27 4LE
Tel: 01323 832083
www.rural.missions.org.uk/sunrise

Scripture Union
207–209 Queensway
Bletchley
Milton Keynes
MK2 2EB
Tel: 01908 856000
www.scriptureunion.org.uk

Children and childhood

Celebrating Children, ed. Miles & Wright, Paternoster 2003
Constructing and Reconstructing Childhood, ed. A. James & A. Prout, Routledge 1997
Childhood Studies, ed. J. and R. Mills, Routledge 2000
Children and Bereavement, Wendy Duffy, CHP 2003
Grandma's Party, Meg Harper, BRF 2003
Special Children; Special Needs, Simon Bass, CHP 2003

Evangelism among children

Every Child—a Chance to Choose, Penny Frank, CPAS 2002
Mission Possible, David Gatward, SU 2001
Seen and Heard, Jackie Cray, Monarch 1995

Spirituality and faith sharing

Children Finding Faith, Francis Bridger, SU 2000
Colours of God, Diana Murrie, BRF 2003
God, Kids and Us, J.M. Eibner & S.G. Walker, Morehouse1997
Godly Play, Jerome W. Berryman, Augsburg 1991
Looking Beyond, Jill Fuller, Kevin Mayhew 1996
Love is Full of Surprises, Jenny Hyson, BRF 2000
Offering the Gospel to Children, G. Wolff Pritchard, Cowley 1992
The 'E' Book, Gill Ambrose, NS/CHP 2000

Worship

101 Ideas for Creative Prayers, Judith Merrell, SU 2001
Launchpad, Neil Pugmire and Mark Rodel, BRF 2004
Lion Book of First Prayers, Su Box, Lion 1998
My Book of Special Times with God, Anne Faulkner, BRF 2002

My Communion Book, Steve Pearce & Diana Murrie, CHP 1997
Poems and Prayers for a Better World, Su Box, Lion 2000
The Communion Cube, Diana Murrie & Margaret Withers, CHP 2003
The Gospels Unplugged, Lucy Moore, BRF 2002
The Lord's Prayer Cube, Diana Murrie, CHP 2004
The Lord's Prayer Unplugged, Lucy Moore, BRF 2004

Children's leaders' handbooks

Become Like a Child, Kathryn Copsey, SU 1994
Children and the Gospel, Ron Buckland, SU 2000
Fired Up... Not Burnt Out, Margaret Withers, BRF 2001
Guide to Building a Team, Andy Back, Children's Ministry 2003
Leading Children, Penny Frank, CPAS 1998
Teaching Godly Play, Jerome W. Berryman, Abingdon 1995

Small groups

Small Groups Growing Churches, Mike Law, SU 2003
Two and Three Together, Margaret Withers, CHP 2004

Children under five

Easy Ways to Bible Fun for the Very Young, Vicki Howie, BRF 2001
Easy Ways to Seasonal Fun for the Very Young, Vicki Howie, BRF 2001
Sharing Jesus with Under Fives, Janet Gaukroger, Crossway 1994
Talking Together: The Christian Year with Under Fives, Patricia Beall Gavigan, Cassell 1996
The Big Red Book: Outlines for Pre-Schools, Ro Willoughby, SU 2001
The Little Red Book: First Steps in Bible Reading, Ro Willoughby, SU 2001
Under Fives—Alive and Kicking!, Jane Farley, Eileen Goddard & Judy Jarvis, CHP 1998

Schools

Linking Churches and Schools, Gillian Wood, CTE 2003

Maximus Mouse and Friends, Brian Ogden, SU 2001
Stay Cool in School, Margaret Goldthorpe, BRF 2003
Stories to Teach about God, Sylvia Green, BRF 2004
Year-Round Assemblies, Brian Ogden, BRF 2002

Holiday club programmes

Champions, John Hardwick, BRF 2004
Out of the Toybox, John Hardwick et al, BRF 2002
Seaside Rock, Dave Chapman, SU 2003
We're Going on a Jungle Jamboree, John Hardwick, BRF 2003
Xpedition Force, Doug Swanney, SU 2004

Fun day materials

Bible Make and Do (Books 1–4), Gillian Chapman, BRF 2003
Celebrations Make and Do, Gillian Chapman, BRF 2004
Easter Make and Do, Gillian Chapman, BRF 2004
Over 300 Games for All Occasions, Patrick Goodland, SU 2002
Theme Games 2, Lesley Pinchback, SU 2003

Midweek ministry

77 Talks for Cyberspace Kids, Chris Chesterton & David Ward, Monarch 2002
After Hours, Rob Hurd, Kevin Mayhew 2003
Building New Bridges, Claire Gibb, NS/CHP 1996
Fuzion—Programme, Mark Griffiths, Monarch 2002
Impact—Programme, Mark Griffiths, Monarch 2003
It's Raining Cats and Dogs… and Elephants?, P. & S. Chapman, Kevin Mayhew 2003
Living in a Fragile World, Peter Privett, BRF 2003
Not Just Sunday, Margaret Withers, CHP 2002
The Adventures of the J Team, Neil Pugmire, BRF 2003

INDEX OF SUBJECTS

INDEX OF BIBLE REFERENCES